LOVE'S

S T R A T E G Y

LOVE'S
STRATEGY

The Political Theology of
Johann Baptist Metz

EDITED BY
JOHN K. DOWNEY

TRINITY PRESS INTERNATIONAL
Harrisburg, Pennsylvania

Trinity Press International, P.O. Box 1321, Harrisburg, PA 17105
Trinity Press International is a division of the Morehouse Group.

Library of Congress Cataloging-in-Publication Data

Love's strategy : the political theology of Johann Baptist Metz /
    edited by John K. Downey.
        p.   cm.
    Includes bibliographical references and index.
    ISBN 13: 978-1-56338-285-7
    1. Metz, Johannes Baptist, 1928-   . 2. Political theology.
    I. Downey, John K., 1948-   .
    BX4705.M545L68   1999
    261.7'092 – dc21   99-40925

Printed in the United States of America

99   00   01   02   03   04   10   9   8   7   6   5   4   3   2   1

Contents

Part 3
HOPING AGAINST HOPE

Acknowledgments

Good theology and good teaching are collaborative. Since this book grows out of my teaching, I acknowledge first the insight and stimulation I have drawn from students. With this book we welcome others to our conversation about political theology. This collection, culled from articles and presentations addressed to various audiences over the years, is not in strictly chronological order. I have left the texts in their original form, editing only for typographical and grammatical slips. Many of these texts were translated before gender-inclusive language became the standard of the profession. It is my hope that readers of a book on political theology will understand the limitations of an earlier social context and read in the inclusive adjustments that certainly reflect the agenda of political theology.

I have consistently found that the words and images of Metz capture the imaginations of diverse readers. These readings have survived undergraduate courses, graduate seminars, and parish adult education groups; all of these learners brought an enthusiasm and a sense of questioning to these texts. Thanks as well to Dr. Hal Rast of Trinity Press International for his commitment to making political theology more available. For her patience and technical aplomb in the mystical mechanics of collecting and reproducing the texts, I thank Fawn Gass of Gonzaga University Faculty Services. The gracious editing and supportive conversation of Alexis A. Nelson have made this a better book. An adult discussion series held at the Francis-Ignatius Center in Spokane, especially the reflections of Jim Snider and Bill Niggemeyer, inspired this publication. Finally, I thank Johann Baptist Metz for his personal support and good humor.

JMII

Introduction

Risking Memory

Political Theology as Interruption

"Be prepared to give an account of the hope that is in you" (1 Pet. 3:15). While Metz doesn't label this his definition of theology, it is the controlling image for his task. The key image for our religious experience is our hope, our grounded imagining of a new political, cultural, economic world that in God's embrace expects justice and honors our common humanity without smoothing over our differences and disagreements. Because this theology describes a hope with its feet on the ground, a worldly hope, it must be a social critique of the world. Political theology calls for all theology to be political, to engage the concrete human world with its social relations, cultural justifications, economic positioning, and all the rest.

The work of Johann Baptist Metz looks especially to those issues theologians call "fundamental" or "foundational": the issues of how we can honestly converse, of establishing the rules of the game in theological discussion. When is a theology good — whether we agree with it or not — and when is it just pious gassing? What is the point of theology? What difference does it make? For Metz the root of these questions and the measure of their tentative answers is our hope. It may be intellectually mediated in a theology or pastorally mediated in the church. And that is why we need both: together they make a home for an impossible hope.

We fundamental theologians must give an account of our hope. So it is very clear that the hope is not the account and that our religious experience is not congruent with the academic investigation or explanation of it. Our task is the intellectual appropriation and defense of our hope.

The account theologians must give is not only an intellectual accounting but, for Metz, a personal accounting as well. What have we done differently because of our hope? How has our theology been a party to our hope? Ours is a hope within and in spite of our broken world, a blemished world theologians must address. How do we address this as theologians? Does theological work, no matter how technical or removed from direct pastoral practice, touch the suffering of humankind? Metz

1

insists that touching the victims is not only part of pastoral care but also a grounding for intellectual discourse, a source for doing academic theology. For Metz, engaging the foundations means giving a religiously and intellectually faithful account of our hope.

Christian religion should challenge whatever ignores the "potholes in hope"; Christian theology should interrupt any ignoring of human suffering, all suppression of human value. Without the edges of both grief and hope, theology becomes banal. It ceases to be the praxis of discipleship and becomes instead a mere ornament that sacralizes the structures of power and control bent on crushing human dignity and hope. Discipleship is praxis, the thoughtful, value-laden enacting of love. Without a concrete strategy, however, love and hope are shapeless. They become merely-believed-in discipleship, merely-believed-in love, and merely-believed-in hope. So much in our culture encourages us to continue doing business as usual while speaking of Christian love. But Christian love takes sides, it judges, it acts for and against. It is easy to forget our call to be and to authorize others to be full, free, human persons.

Reading Metz: What to Expect

Metz writes fundamental theology. This means the reader can't expect him to lay out a systematic picture of various doctrines. He wants to lay the foundations for doing theology, to address the more basic rules of the game, to remind us of the questions that ground systematic reflection. Questions are an essential mark of theology, which is today more about questioning than answering. Metz wants to give an orientation, not a box of positions. He offers instead vectors of thought that readers draw into their own particular circumstances. Political theology as foundational theology is, then, a portable perspective and a pattern of questioning.

Metz's goal is to shape our inquiring. His writing style reflects his subject: using an unusual number of questions in his writing, he continually puts the burden on us, pushing us to imagine things differently and to form a reflective response. Readers will not find here, then, fully developed systems, but rather reminders, markers, hints, and interruptions. Metz is deliberate in this style and in his avoidance of systematizing. A system gives the impression that theory has resolved the critical questions and quelled the dialectic. Furthermore, being too systematic would involve too grave a set of risks: a false universalism, an absorption of real but untoward particulars, and a flattening of the peculiar existential context. Metz doubts that he could produce the final theology for every culture or every age from his desk in Münster. He sees rather that contemporary theologies will vary with their context or with actual problems addressed; though they might agree on the sorts of moves to be made, those actual moves must be colored by various venues. Political theology is not a doctrine but an ongoing and open-ended project of engagement. Metz offers not a map but a compass by which to negotiate our engagement. So, in reading Metz, be prepared for an unsystematic "feel" to the materials and for the consequent chance to think through the issue. How Metz writes is a part of what he is communicating, for political theology is about taking responsibility — even on the level of style.

Metz refers to his theology as a *practical* fundamental theology. Human beings think, and eventually they will need to think about religion. Religious practice and theology certainly overlap: the many practices and doctrines we learn as children began as theological innovations or as fallout from serious disagreement in the community. But while our Christianity is rooted in stories — Metz reminds us that theological notions of God are shorthand for the stories of exodus, conversion, resistance, and suffering — practical fundamental theology is not these stories. It protects these stories from distortion and reclaims doctrines as challenging, even dangerous memories. While theology functions by the argument and evidence of the intellectual life as normed by the community of inquirers, it must be practical. It is not an innovation to claim that Christians should pay attention to Matthew 25 and love one another, but it *is* different to insist that these practical imperatives be integrated as the intellectual foundation for doing technical theology. The standard for intellectual truth is now not only coherence but transformation, not only right talking but right acting, not only orthodoxy but orthopraxy.

Much of contemporary theology seems incredible, a boring and irrelevant clash of jargons signifying nothing. Does one's theology make a difference to the world? Our present situation is one in which values seem market-driven and traditions ossified. Nevertheless, for Metz, Christianity and theology are fabulous resources for resistance and hope. Political theology is not just another "genitive" theology, a theology "of" something. It is not the application of an already worked-out theory to various other areas, in this case, the area of politics. Rather, it is a redesigning of all theological questioning to be sensitive to the social, economic, and political values that accompany all human enterprises. Political theology thus understood contributes to the transformation of the world. Ours is a culture of amnesia, and political theology is a countercultural antidote of remembrance. Political theology is love's strategy.

Though Metz's project is inherently unsystematic, it may be helpful to evoke the sensibility within which his theology moves. Among the chords Metz favors in his writing are these: theology as mystical and political,

evolutionary apathy and the apocalyptic, human suffering, and the call
to be subjects.

Theology as Mystical and Political

A Christian theology must be *both* mystical and political. A theology that
is only mystical falls short of the Christian standard, as does a theology
that is only political. Experience teaches that a politics without any sense
of transcendent value has often been fatal to human dignity, and a Christianity that doesn't touch our sociopolitical selves forgets the Crucified
One and becomes soporific and noxious. The overlap of the political and
mystical, then, is essential to the Christian perspective.

Does Metz mean we must all become mystics? No, we are not all called
to the direct and intense experience reported by the likes of John of Cross
or Teresa of Avila; however, we are all called to touch our experience of
God — even if our experience is largely a questioning directed to God.
Theology cares about the experience of transcendence, and the Christian
experience of transcendence is entwined with prophetic critique. Christians are called to yoke the spiritual and the social. And so for Metz,
Christianity is a world religion in which one may be *too* mystical.

Metz wants to deprivatize our religion and our theology. Reducing
Christian mysticism to the sphere of so-called private existence is not
only naive but also dangerous, for it reduces discipleship to a matter of
personal style or preference. It reverses the Incarnation by removing Jesus
from our world. Authentic Christianity is a public mysticism.

Does Metz mean we must all become politicians or social workers?
No, far from it. Metz uses the word "political" to remind us to attend
to concrete social circumstances. He doesn't use the word "political" to
refer to the process of electing a mayor or the parties who run a government. He uses it more in the sense of the *polis*, the community of human
beings acting in especially human ways. His usage indicates a sensitivity to the social, economic, and cultural values present in any situation.
Human life is value laden, and this theology simply asks what sort of
person those deep values reflect and create. What is our responsibility?

We have lost our innocence today: we know from the explosion in
social sciences as well as contemporary hermeneutical (interpretation)
theory that our theories, actions, and reconstructions are not innocent.
Those "Masters of Suspicion" — Freud, Marx, and Nietzsche — have
shown that there might be a hidden agenda in human thought and action.
It may not always be a bad agenda, but we know it might be there:
concerns about sex or death, about class and economics, about power
and domination. We are no longer innocent of the fact that invisible

vectors of power and interest can drive our lives. We realize today more than ever before that there are good reasons why we do things and then there are the real reasons. This loss of innocence is precisely why we need a theology that is political, that is, one that pays self-conscious attention to these issues. This is a theology of the world, a theology for mature people who live in that world, a theology of social critique that helps people answer the Christian call to social responsibility.

Evolutionary Apathy and Apocalyptic Time

Time directs a life. When time is limited, action grows more urgent, priorities emerge, and decisions become meaningful. (Perhaps Calypso envied Odysseus.) When time is unlimited, forever more of the same, then life too becomes a pointless trajectory. Time with a limit is time that pressures us to act and to take care in acting before it is too late. Metz reminds us that Christian time not only has an end, it has a finale.

The biblical God is not a tentative hypothetical presence. From Genesis to The Apocalypse the biblical God acts in definite times, places, and persons. So history is not the sweep of grand impersonal cycles, not the turning of a giant wheel: it is a narrative. Only when time is delimited does it make sense to say that there will be justice, that God vindicates the victims, that promises will be kept, that this action matters. The end of time is not as frightening as endless time.

Geological time can be depressing. Consider the vast years, billions of them, the various epochs of cosmic evolution. Astronauts have brought back 4.9-billion-year-old rocks from our moon. *Homo erectus* was lumbering along 1.7 million years ago, and the earliest *homo sapiens* claims a mere 600,000 years of history. Within all of this expanse of time, what is one person's life? A bit of dust on a cockroach's rump — a roach whose descendants may be there long after us. If this is so, what is the point of acting? If the space of our paltry lives is so insignificant, how can those lives make any difference? Or worse, are we just microscopic bits of flotsam in a vast mechanical process? Evolutionary time can tempt us to deny any human claims on each other: why not kick back, turn on the game, and pour another drink? But Christian memory tweaks us from this comfortable rest. Time has a direction. The last judgment, the parousia, the promises of God are about the claims which fall upon us as followers of Christ — now. We are called to live up to the expectations of God!

Metz is concerned with evolutionary apathy and with reclaiming our apocalyptic traditions as an antidote to that apathy. He does not worry about Darwin nor does he turn to the Four Horsemen of the Apocalypse to kill conversation. Catholics — theologians and their pope — do not reject evolutionary theory. They complement it or integrate it into their vision, but they do not simply drive around it by denying it. The contemporary problem is not evolution but using evolution as an alibi for sloth. The apocalyptic threads of our tradition insist that how we have acted within our time does make a difference. Consider the judgment scene of Matt. 25:31–45 in which the damned must answer for their failure to act. Or the earlier parable of the ten maidens with their lamps who know not when the bridegroom is coming but must be ready.

Metz is no ahistorical fundamentalist spotting the Antichrist among liberal politicians or claiming the predictive accuracy of the Book of Revelation: he is after the urgency of human behavior in the light of Christian hope. The Apocalypse reveals hope and justice for an oppressed, occupied, and depressed people. And today, we too drift into frustration, cycles of seemingly intractable social decline, a shower of social surds, shock, despair, inaction. But there is hope. For Christians time is not a bland and infinite continuum. Rather, time has a finale: it is going somewhere. When an end is in view, that end acts as a lure and a motive, orienting us amid the sadness and chaos. And God's definitive revelation in Jesus makes demands: responsibilities beckon.

The Call to Be "Subjects"

There are demands upon us. While we cannot control all that happens to us, neither are we mere puppets of history, standing by in the midst of its overwhelming waves. We are expected to take responsibility for our lives. To say it in theological shorthand: God calls us to be "subjects." For Metz, a subject is not just a lone individual; rather, the subject is the individual in the weave of community. "Subject" comes to indicate a person of responsibility, a person tied to humanity. This call to be subjects entails a call to honor and to empower others as subjects. Our very connectedness makes claims on us, and Christians are called to show their connection in their actions: to be doers, actors, subjects, agents, and not mere passive objects bobbing atop the waters of history. The fully human person — the subject — is a person of *praxis*. Subjects are called to act in human, value-laden ways that honor the human good.

Metz's focus on the praxis of authentic subjects helps political theology develop a nontheoretical standard for understanding, judging, and acting. The history of this Greek term from Aristotle to neo-Marxism need not concern us here. Suffice it to say that people use this term to evoke a human experience that is more than a theory and more than simply any practice. Too often an elegant theory can hide human destructiveness or become a tool of oppression. Praxis is doing inherently human actions, ones that automatically stress human value such as creating human relation, connecting ourselves to others and honoring them. Metz's use of the term focuses on the call to be truly human subjects, and it puts an edge of resistance on his theology. Praxis points out that Christians must be driven by transformative action and not by any conceptual package. But this human doing is thoughtful: praxis is *informed, thoughtful, humane* doing. It is action and reflection in a continuous feedback loop with action as the ultimate criterion for truth.

So-called realists might ask whether banking on the human response to praxis and the call to be subjects is naive or utopian. Political theology does have hope in the responsiveness of humankind, but this hope is compounded of a hope in God. Thomas More invented the word *utopia* as a play on two Greek words, each based on the root for "place" (*topos*) and the fact that the *u* prefix might be either Greek for "good" (*eu*) or Greek for "no" (*ou*). So *utopia* might mean either "no place" or "a good place." Metz's hopes are not idealistic illusions fastened on "no place," on a place that could never be. Rather they are quite realistic expectations for a full life, hoping against hope because we are not alone: we find God, Hopkins knows, "deep down things." Christians expect more of humankind because God expects more.

The future for which we strive need not be drawn in detailed, shared photographs. We have ways of knowing it from its negative: we do know where and when it is not. The suffering of the tortured cries out to us no matter how loudly others proclaim ideologies, policies, and reason. When Christians hear that in theory it may sometimes be good for one man to die for the people, they feel uneasy, not calm: this is what those plotting against Jesus said. One need not limn the blueprint for a better society or economics in order to see the suffering of victims. Talk of freedom, praxis, and subjectivity without attention to their concrete absence in social and political structures is unrealistic and untethered, a mere battle of words.

When praxis fades, when we become less than subjects, when we become dehumanized, devalued, and shrunken, we touch a fundamental common human experience: suffering. Suffering is the touchstone that connects us and reorients us. This common thread in human experience reveals the denigration of the subject. Not only is the authority of those who suffer universal, but it is difficult for any theoretical or interpretative sleight-of-hand to supersede this authority. Suffering is the starting point for dialogue across cultures, religions, and histories. Here is the foundation for theological conversation. Praxis and suffering are not just about knowing we are linked together: they are also about actively seeking the human good. It is not just that we recognize the fact of our interconnectedness, but that we feel the claim of those others upon us. Praxis and suffering anchor discussions across borders and keep us honest: facing those who suffer and have suffered is a sobering call to act.

Theology must — in its internal norms and foundations and not just in its applications — help to change the pattern of domination and suffering in this world. Hypothetical, coherent elegance is important, but only as normed by transforming activity. (Theology helps us take responsibility for our hope) Theoretical issues help us maintain and grasp our Christian hope, but finally Christianity is not primarily concerned with theoretical issues. Any Christian orthodoxy must true itself in Christian orthopraxy. So theology is judged by its contribution to the transformation of human life.

Remember and Resist

Political theology is not a doctrine but a task and an ongoing project. It is not another theory, but an interruption. This theology turns around resistance and memory. We must resist the current of domination that washes over us and resist its siren call to dominate others. We recall and connect to suffering and we remember God's demand that we exercise and empower praxis. But such a memory can disrupt the status quo, cast a shadow on business as usual, and arm the victims. We must remember our grief and our hope.

(For Metz the categories of theology are memory, solidarity, and narrative. *Memoria passionis*, the memory of suffering, is our critical tool for survival: it is a dangerous memory.) The Christian memory of suffering is dangerous because it warns us where things have gone wrong and challenges our comfort in the official story. The memory of suffering, our own and especially that of others, connects each with the other and provides a practical warning system about distorted relationships, institutions, and situations. Indeed, the story of Jesus itself is a story of a good man killed by political and religious leaders. Christians who remember can never blindly trust their religious and political leaders. It could happen again. And this memory impels us to a solidarity with victims. This solidarity also safeguards our praxis; the view from the underside of history challenges us to act in empathetic connection to those who suffer. We must act and do theology while touching victims. All of this requires a commitment to narrative: in narrative we remember and reconnect. By participating in a narrative we trade experiences with others. This keeps memory and solidarity alive. Metz's political theology provides the lenses of memory, of solidarity, and of narrative so that we can look at our world and act in ways that bring more abundant life. This new canon for the intellectual work of theology is political, yet mystical; it touches human suffering, honors others, and feels the pressure of God's time. It calls us to remember and resist.

(An image may be useful in conveying the texture of the political theologian's perspective. Metz tells the German folktale about the race between the hare and the hedgehog. The hedgehog was rather vain and proud of his legs. One day the hare happened to make fun of him and so the hedgehog challenged the hare to a race. The race course — two furrows — allowed no one to actually see the runners. The hedgehog asked to go home first and eat. While at home he got his wife, who was identical to him, dressed her in the same clothes he was wearing, and stationed her at the end of the furrow. When the hare said, "Go!" the hedgehog just ducked down in place while his wife popped up at the finish line with "I'm already here!" The story shows us that the weak can challenge the strong if they use their heads. But Metz wants to tell the story against the grain ("against the quills," as he says.)He wants us to model our theology on the hare and not the hedgehog. The hare really enters the race of human history and runs for all he's worth. The hedgehog merely pretends to run: he actually remains at rest. Talking a good game, the hedgehog goes around concrete history. For Metz, too much of our theology has been a hedgehog trick: talking about history, but never mentioning the suffering, the losers, the horrors. A glib joy and hope, a theoretical, already-won salvation history constructed with our backs to Auschwitz cannot confront the horrors of history. Metz calls for us to enter that real history, which is also the history of suffering, the history that needs us, the history that puts a claim on us to act. The fact the Jesus suffered and died does not put us at ease, but charges us with taking him and those like him off the cross. In Münster over the desk of Johann Baptist Metz hangs a very large picture of a hare running at full speed.

Biographical Note

Johann Baptist Metz (b. August 5, 1928) is a Roman Catholic diocesan priest from Bavaria (Auerbach). He is Ordinary Professor of Fundamental Theology, Emeritus, at Westphalian Wilhelms University in the northern German town of Münster. He was until recently Visiting Lecturer in Politics and Religion at the Institute for Philosophy at the University of Vienna. His books include *Poverty of Spirit, The Emergent Church, Faith in History and Society: Toward a Practical Fundamental Theology*, and *Hope Against Hope: Johann Baptist Metz and Elie Wiesel Speak Out on the Holocaust*. He is a founding editor of *Concilium*. Two recent collections of his articles are *Faith and the Future: Essays on The-*

ology, Solidarity and Modernity (with Jürgen Moltmann) and *A Passion for God: The Mystical-Political Dimension of Christianity* — which also has a good general bibliography.

Suggested Background Reading

Ashley, J. Matthew. *Interruptions: Mysticism, Politics and Theology in the Work of Johann Baptist Metz.* Notre Dame, Ind.: University of Notre Dame Press, 1998.

Chopp, Rebecca S. "Political Theology." *The Praxis of Suffering: An Interpretation of Liberation and Political Theologies,* 28–45. Maryknoll, N.Y.: Orbis, 1986.

———. "The Subject of Suffering." In Chopp, *Praxis of Suffering,* 64–81.

Lamb, Matthew L. "Political Theology." In *The New Dictionary of Theology,* ed. Joseph A. Komonchak, Mary Collins, and Dermot A. Lane, 772–79. Wilmington, Del.: Michael Glazier, 1988.

———. "Praxis." In *New Dictionary of Theology,* ed. Komonchak, Collins, and Lane, 784–87.

Lane, Dermot A. "The Move to Praxis in Theology." *Foundations for a Social Theology: Praxis, Process, and Salvation,* 6–31. New York: Paulist Press, 1984.

Omerod, Neil. "Johann Baptist Metz, *Political Theology.*" *Introducing Contemporary Theologies: The What and Who of Theology Today,* 124–33. Maryknoll, N.Y.: Orbis, 1997.

Ostovich, Steven T. "Political Theology in Interdisciplinary Dialogue." *Reason in History: Theology and Science as Community Activities,* 97–125. Atlanta: Scholars Press, 1990.

———. "The Political Theology of J. B. Metz." In Ostovich, *Reason in History,* 33–95.

Part 1

The Future Church

Chapter 1

The Church and the World

If the precise point of view from which this subject will be treated here is to be clear, some preliminary remarks are needed.

First: For the theologian councils are never an end, with which he can be content, but rather a beginning. They bring forth new tasks and, consequently, do not diminish, but increase theological responsibility. Therefore, although we may admire the progress made by the Second Vatican Council, we should not overlook its limitations and its contingent character. For example, did not the Church in this Council speak too exclusively of herself, in a narcissistic way, looking into a mirror, rather than through an open window into the world, to find her true countenance? Moreover, since the Church has evidently not spoken of everything of which she could have and should have spoken, it would be false and dangerous if theologians would limit themselves during the next fifty years to a mere commentary on the various constitutions of this Council. For this reason, my remarks on "The Church and the World" will concentrate not so much on what the Council said as on what the Council did *not* say.

The second preliminary remark relates directly to our topic and its scope. Since the extensive scope of this topic can easily lead to superficiality, I will limit my treatment in two ways. The first limitation results from the fact that I write as a professor of fundamental theology. This discipline serves the responsibility of hope according to 1 Pet. 3:15: "Always be prepared to make a defense to anyone who calls you to account for the hope that is in you." Thus fundamental theology seeks to explicate the faith in a manner corresponding to the present historical modes of human understanding. It does this not in order to submit itself to the ruling modes of thought, but in order to enter into a fruitful conflict with these modes of thought. I will therefore treat this topic of "The Church and the World" as a problem that belongs to the responsibility of the Christian faith as confronted with the present historical situation and its modes of thought. The usual conflict between the thought of the times and the thought of the Christian faith often forces the individual Christian to walk through the crucial tests of his faith alone and without the adequate help of theology for his present situation.

The second limitation of my treatment results from the horizon[1] in which I would like to explain and to develop concretely the relation of the Christian faith to the world. This horizon is the future. And it reveals the world as history, history as final history (*Endgeschichte*), faith as hope, and theology as eschatology. This horizon characterizes the attempt of theology to surpass and to go beyond the modern transcendental, personalistic, and existential theology without disregarding its valuable insights. This transcendental, personalistic, and existential theology has correctly emphasized the role of the human person in contrast to the mere objectivistic viewpoint of scholastic theology. It has brought the Christian faith into a proper relationship to human existence and subjectivity. However, this theology faces two dangers. On the one hand, this anthropological theology tends to limit the faith by concentrating on the *actual* moment of the believer's personal decision. The *future* is then all but lost. It becomes only another name for the intractable factors of the present decision. On the other hand, this anthropological theology tends to become private and individualistic. It fails to bring into sufficient prominence the social and political dimensions of the believer's faith and responsibility.

After these preliminary remarks, we turn to our topic, "The Church and the World." I would like to develop three theses: First, a thesis on the modern understanding of the world, with its stress on the future and its operational orientation. Second, a thesis on the scriptural source of our understanding of the world, an understanding rooted in the promises of God. Third, a thesis on the resulting notion of faith as a creative and militant relationship to the world understood in the light of God's promises.

I

First thesis: The modern man's understanding of the world is fundamentally oriented toward the future. His mentality therefore is not primarily contemplative but operative.

First of all, the modern era persistently strives after the New (*das Novum*). This era began with the "new" world and this new world stamped the slogan of its program on the dollar bill: "*Novus* ordo seclorum." This striving after the new is the predominate spirit of the social, political, and technical revolutions of our time. The men of this era are

---

1. Cf. K. Rahner, "Theology and Anthropology," in *The Word in History*, ed. T. Patrick Burke (New York: Sheed and Ward, 1966), 23 n. 1.

attracted and fascinated *only* by the future, that is, by that which has never been. "This fascination with the future transforms the existing and subsisting reality into a changing and a challenging reality, so that the real of this reality emerges as its possibilities for the future."[2]

Since the modern man's "passion is for the possible" (Kierkegaard), the direct force of tradition has declined. The old quickly turns into the obsolete. "The good old days" have lost their appeal. The golden age lies not behind us, but before us: it is not re-created in the memories of our dreams, but created in the desires of our imagination and heart. Man's relationship to the past becomes increasingly a mere esthetic, romantic, and archaic interest, and by his archival curiosity for the past he acknowledges the past as something antiquated. In other words, the present mentality has a merely historical (*historisch*) relationship to the past, but it has an existential (*geschichtlich*) relationship to the future.

Second: In his striving toward the future the modern man no longer experiences the world as an imposed fate, or as a sovereign sacrosanct nature confining him, but rather as a quarry "as the raw material" — with which he builds his own "new world." He not only alters the world and forms it into the stage props for his own historical drama, but he also dominates the world through technology, and thereby secularizes it.[3]

Third: How should theology relate itself to this new world situation? Some theologians play the ostrich and wish for the situation to pass. Others have taken the situation seriously and used various forms of dialectical theology to relate Christianity and the world (especially students and friends of Karl Barth: e.g., F. Gogarten and D. Bonhoeffer). Since the new understanding of the world has questioned and even thrown away many of the tried and faithful thought-forms of the Christian faith, these perceptive theologians emphasize the radical otherness of the faith — its radical difference from this world. And in this paradoxical understanding of the Christian faith by the modern theologies of secularization, dialectical theology celebrates a victory in the theology of secularization. For example, the use of the dialectical theology of Barth, Gogarten, and Bonhoeffer gives evidence to its ambiguous character in Harvey Cox's important book, *The Secular City*. He attempts in the first part to emphasize the total transcendence and otherness of God and the Christian faith, and in the second part of his book to unite eschatology and social revolution. But, I ask, how can the gospel of the totally other God flow

---

2. Gerhard Ebeling, *Wort and Glaube* (Tübingen: J. C. B. Mohr [Paul Siebeck], 1962), 387.

3. Cf. Johannes B. Metz, "Zukunft des Glaubens in einer hominisierten Welt," in *Weltverständnis im Glauben*, ed. Johannes Metz (Mainz: Matthias-Grünewald, 1965), 452.

into a social gospel: in other words, how does Cox unite the first and second part of his book?[4]

In order to demonstrate the insufficiency of this reaction of "dialectical theology" we will examine in a more precise manner what has actually occurred in the modern age's new understanding of the world. The "World-Beyond" (*Jenseits*) and the "Heaven above us" have not only become hidden, but seem to have disappeared. (What is hidden can indeed be powerful and near!) Slowly but constantly the world has lost its glimmer of divinity: we have this world in our hands and projects. No longer is the world recognized as the numinous vestibule of heaven. No longer do we directly discover in and on the world the footsteps of God, the *vestigia Dei*, but rather we see only the footsteps of men, the *vestigia hominis*, and *his* actions of changing the world. We apparently encounter in and on the world only ourselves and our own possibilities. The shining glow of the "world above" and the "world beyond" has dimmed. It seems as if it can no longer enlighten the spirit of man and enkindle his enthusiasm. What moves the man of today is not the commitment for the "world above" but the commitment to build a *new* world (or, if you will, to build a "great society"). This engagement and commitment to the future does challenge and appeal to the man of today, who otherwise seems so disenchanted and so areligious.

Fourth: Both in the West and the East every impressive *Weltanschauung* and humanistic ideology of today is oriented toward the future. We need only to think about Marxism and its theory of the classless society, according to which man himself produces his own future and society: The desired perfection of a successful mankind does not lie "above us" but "before us." The total modern critique against religion, beginning with the Marxist critique, can be reduced to this common denominator: Christianity, as well as religion in general, is powerless in the face of this primacy which the future occupies in the modern mentality. Our present age is therefore conceived of by these critics as the time of the liquidation of the religious mentality, as the beginning of a postreligious era, in which every belief in a transcendent God is exposed as a mere speculative conception of the mind, to be cast off and replaced by an active and operative orientation toward the future.

Fifth: What does the Christian faith say or do in the face of this situation? How does the Christian account for *his* hope? Can he understand the world in a way that does not flatly exclude his faith, that does not force his theology into an irrelevant and incomprehensible paradox? Can

---

4. Cf. Francis Fiorenza, "Säkularisation und die säkularisierte Stadt," *Stimmen der Zeit* (May 1966).

the Christian faith perhaps find itself *anew* in this situation and *grow* in the midst of making the world? I believe it can, but under one condition: only if the Christian theologian becomes alarmed about a loss of eschatology, and only if he becomes disturbed about the neglect and unawareness of the future in his theology. This neglect is so persistent that, for example, the so-called *existential* interpretation of the New Testament involves only the reactualization and the re-presentation of the past in the present moment of religious decision. The present alone dominates. There is no real future! *Exempli gratia:* Bultmann! We must bring together that which has been so long disastrously separated: namely Transcendence (God) and Future, because this orientation toward the future is demanded by the biblical faith and message itself. Only then can the faith enter into a fruitful conflict and discussion with our modern era's passion for the future. Only a theology which has repossessed its orientation to the future can seriously ask: where does this primacy of the future come from, which primacy impregnates the modern mentality and the political, social, and technical revolutions of our times? What is the origin of this primacy of the future? What is its foundation?[5]

II

Second thesis: The orientation of the modern era to the future, and the understanding of the world as history, which results from this orientation, is based upon the biblical belief in the promises of God. This biblical faith demands that theology be eschatology.

I can naturally give only a few explanatory comments to this thesis. My direct appeal to the statements of the sacred scriptures is not arbitrary, but is based upon the results of recent biblical research in Germany, which in its post-Bultmannian period is bringing back into focus the Old Testament, and, second, is using the Old Testament as a means of understanding the New Testament.

First of all, recent exegetical researches indicate that the words of Revelation in the Old Testament are not primarily words of statement or of information, nor are they mainly words of appeal or of personal self-communication by God, but they are *words of promise.* Their statement is announcement, their announcement is proclamation of what is to come, and therefore the abrogation of what is. (Perhaps the German would more clearly express my thought: *Die Aussage ist Ansage, die Verkündigung ist Ankündigung des Kommenden und dadurch Auf-*

---

5. Cf. Johann B. Metz, "Gott vor uns," in *Ernst Bloch zu Ehren* (Frankfurt: Suhrkamp Verlag, 1965), 227–41.

kündigung des Bestehenden.) This dominant proclamation and word of promise initiates the future: it establishes the covenant as the solidarity of the Israelites who hope, and who thereby experience the world for the first time as a history which is oriented to the future. This Hebrew experience and thought stand in contrast to Greek thought, which understands the world not as a history oriented to the future, but as a closed cosmos or as a subsisting world of nature. This Hebrew thought is contained in those important passages of the Old Testament which are impregnated with a pathos for the new (*das Novum*), for the new time and for the new coming world, that is, for the new as that which *never* was. Greek thought, in contrast to Hebrew thought,[6] considers that which has never been as intrinsically impossible, since for the Greeks there is "nothing new under the sun." Everything which will come in the future is only a variation of the past and an actualization or confirmation of the *anamnesis*. History is therefore only the indifferent return of the same within the closed realm of the eternal cosmos. Since the essence of history is here considered as cyclic, history is seen as devouring her own children over and over again, so that there is nothing new in history, and the essence of history reveals itself as nihilistic. We emphasize this contrast between the Hebrew and Greek understanding of the world in order to show that the biblical viewpoint considers the world as a *historical* world, insofar as it is a world "arising toward" God's promises under the responsibility of the Israelites, who hope in these promises. This understanding is reflected in the Genesis creation narratives, which were originally narratives of God's promises (so that they therefore express not merely a faith in a past creation, but a faith in the new creation of God's promises). The revelation of God's name in Exod. 3:14 also indicates that this eschatological horizon is the central aspect of God's revelation. The expression "I am who I am" is much better translated as "I will be who I will be." (So Gerhard van Rad and Martin Buber and a footnote in the RSV.) According to this version God revealed himself to Moses more as the power of the future than as a being dwelling beyond all history and experience. God is not "above us" but "before us." His transcendence reveals itself as our "absolute future." This future is grounded in itself, and is self-possessed. It is a future that is not erected out of the potentialities of our human freedom and human action. Rather, this future calls forth our potentialities to unfold themselves in history. Only such a future — one that is more than just the projections of our abilities — can call us to realize truly *new* possibilities, to become that which has *never* existed. "I will be who I will be." The future proclaimed here does not get its power

---

6. Cf. Johannes B. Metz, "Welt," *Lexicon für Theologie und Kirche,* 10:1027–46.

from our present wishes and efforts.[7] No, its power stems from itself: it belongs to itself. Only thus can and does this future exert its stirring and liberating power over *every* human present, over *every* generation.

Second: The New Testament message does not remove the faith's orientation toward the future or hope in the future as the necessary and essential structure of faith. "The firm belief in the nearness of the Kingdom, which Jesus proclaimed and initiated, effected such a concentration and mobilization toward the promised future, that everything of the mere past and of the mere present lost its relevance."[8]

It would be moreover false to think that in the Christ-Event the future is entirely behind us, as if the future of the history after Christ only plays itself out, but does not *realize* itself. On the contrary, the Christ-Event intensifies this orientation toward the not-yet-realized future. The proclamation of the resurrection of Jesus, which can never be separated from the message of the crucifixion, is essentially a proclamation of promise which initiates the Christian mission. This mission achieves its future insofar as the Christian alters and "innovates" the world toward that future of God which is definitely promised to us in the resurrection of Jesus Christ. The New Testament is therefore centered on hope — a creative expectancy — as the very essence of Christian existence.

Third: In view of the above, the Christian has the responsibility to develop his faith's relationship to the world as a relationship of hope, and to explicate his theology as eschatology. Although theology has a tract on eschatology, it generally puts this eschatology in a corner, well away from the center of theology, in the treatise "on the last things." Eschatology lacks a vital relationship to the whole of theology and it thereby fails to be related to the theology of the world. Christian eschatology must come out of its corner, into which it was shoved by a theology which has forgotten the relevance of hope and of the future. Since Christians are simply defined by Paul as "those who have hope," should they not understand their theology in *every* aspect as eschatology, and as the responsibility of hope? Eschatology is not a discipline beside other disciplines, but that basic discipline which determines, forms, and shapes every theological statement, especially those concerning the world. The attempt to interpret theology in a totally existential or personalistic way is an important accomplishment of theology. I attempted in my *Christliche Anthropozentrik* to base this interpretation upon Thomas Aquinas. This existential-anthropological theology, however, easily becomes isolated from the world and history when eschatology is not seen to be more basic

---

7. Cf. Wolfhart Pannenberg, "Der Gott der Hoffnung," in *Ernst Bloch zu Ehren*, 215.
8. Ibid., 212.

to theology. Only in the eschatological horizon of hope does the world appear as history. Only in the understanding of world as history does the free action of man obtain its central position. Only this central position of human freedom initiates a legitimate Christian anthropocentrism. The universal existential-anthropological viewpoint in the Christian theology depends on the eschatological viewpoint. This is true, because only in the eschatological horizon of hope does the world appear as an *arising* reality, whose development or process is committed to the free action of man. In addition, Christology and Ecclesiology must also be explicated in this horizon of eschatology, so that they are not abbreviated to either mere existential-anthropological or objectivized and cosmological viewpoints. At this point we can only mention these considerations and aspects. We will, however, say a word concerning ecclesiology further below.

Fourth: It would be tempting, and important, to indicate how the process of the so-called secularization of the world was only possible because the world itself was experienced and understood in the eschatological horizon of hope. The world appears in this horizon not as a fixed and sacrosanct reality in a preestablished harmony, but as an *arising* reality, which can be innovated toward its future through the historically free actions of men. This universal alteration and innovation of the world through the offensive of human freedom characterizes that process, which we call secularization. We must, however, pass over our question here and proceed to our next thesis.

III

Third thesis: The relationship between the Christian faith and the world should be characterized from a theological viewpoint as a creative and militant eschatology.

First: In explaining and establishing this thesis we would like to refer to a noteworthy sentence of St. Thomas Aquinas. He states in scholastic terminology that man does not have a natural last end (*finis ultimus naturalis*) and a supernatural last end (*finis ultimus supernaturalis*); but he has *only one* last end, namely, the future promised by God. From the viewpoint of the future the often used — perhaps too often used — distinction between the natural and the supernatural recedes into the background. In our relationship to the future we cannot be satisfied with a distinction which separates the natural future of the world from the supernatural future of the faith and of the Church. Both dimensions converge in our relationship to the future. In other words, since the hope of the Christian faith is orientated toward the future, it cannot fulfill itself in bypassing the world and the future of the world. And because this hope is responsible for the *one* promised future, it is therefore also responsible for the future of the world. The Christian faith hopes not only in itself, the Church hopes not only in itself, but they hope in the world.

Second: Is the biblical hope, however, really so radically orientated toward this one and undivided future? Is the Old Testament's conception of hope as a hope in the world and in its future still valid? Does not the New Testament require that this hope be impregnated with and accompanied by a renunciation of the world? It would indeed be unwise, and an empty compromise with the spirit of the times, if we would suppress or minimize this motif of the New Testament's conception of hope. I am aware of this motif and I consider it important — even for our times. However, everything hinges upon a correct understanding of what is properly meant by the renunciation of the world. Because man can never live apart from the world or be worldless (without a world), this renunciation could never be a mere flight out of the world. For such a flight would then be a deceptive and illusory flight into an artificially isolated world, which de facto is often the more comfortable religious situation of yesterday. Not a flight *out* of the world, but a flight *with* the world "forward" is the fundamental dynamism of the Christian hope in its renunciation of the world. This renunciation is therefore a flight only out of that self-made world which masters its present and lives solely out of its present, and whose "time is always here" (cf. John 7, 6). Christians should attentively listen to Saint Paul when he exhorts them to renounce the world, and when he urges them "not to be conformed to this world" (cf. Romans 12, 2). Paul does not criticize here the Christian's *solidarity* with the world, but his conformity to the existing world as enraptured with its own appearance, and as concerned only with its self-glorification. Paul criticizes this world insofar as it tries to determine its own future and to degrade this future to a function of the powerful and power-hungry present. The Apostle does not demand a one-sided (*undialektisch*) denial of the world or a total refusal of engagement with the world. But rather he urges the Christians to be prepared for a painful estrangement from the present world situation. He exhorts them to renounce the forgone conclusions of their times (cf. also Matt. 12:29ff.) and to abstain from the proud boastfulness and vanity of the world (cf. 1 Cor. 1:29). All of this, however, is done for the sake of that future promised by God. The Christian is moved to flee and to renounce the world not because he despises the world but because he hopes in the future of the world as proclaimed in God's promises. And this hope gives him a responsibility for the world and its future — a future from which we can too often isolate ourselves in forms of presumption and despair. This Christian renunciation of the world has its origin in the spirit of biblical hope and it serves the hope of all. It is the imitation of Christ at the hour of his crucifixion. This hour represents the singular affirmation of the world *and* the overcoming of the world. The Christian renunciation of the world takes on the servant's form of a crucified hope for the world. A faith which is guided by such a hope is primarily not a doctrine, but an initiative for the passionate innovating and changing of the world toward the Kingdom of God.

Third: In this perspective we can more adequately define the relationship between Church and world. Despite the many discussions about the Church and the world, there is nothing more unclear than the nature of their relationship to one another. The usual contemporary statements about the turning of the Church toward the world and about the positive evaluation of the world by the Church, etc., often add to the confusion and unclarity. Is the Church actually something other than the world? Is not the Church also world? Are not Christians — that is, the Church — also of the world? Where is the Church turning to in her movement toward the world? The Church is of the world: In a certain sense the Church is the world: The Church is not nonworld (*Die Kirche ist nicht Nicht-Welt*). For it is *that world* which attempts to live from the promised future of God, and to call *that world* in question which understands itself only in terms of itself and its possibilities. The decisive relationship between the Church and the world is not spatial but temporal. The Church is the eschatological community and the exodus community. Its institutional and sacramental life is based on this eschatological character. The Eucharist is the sacrament of the Exodus; it is the commemoration of the death of Christ *as promise — donec dominus veniat*. The Church is not the goal of her own strivings; this goal is the Kingdom of God. "The Church always lives in a certain sense from the proclamation of her provisional character and from her historically progressive surrender to the coming Kingdom of God."[9] The Church has a hope and witnesses to a hope, but its hope is not in itself. It is rather a hope in the Kingdom of God as the future of the world. *Ecclesia est universale sacramentum spei pro totius mundi salute.*

Fourth: How does the Church realize its mission to work for the future of the world? It cannot be by pure contemplation, since contemplation by definition relates to what has already become existent and to what actually exists. The future which the Church hopes for is not yet here, but is *emerging* and *arising* (*entstehend*). Therefore the hope which the Church sets in itself and in the world should be creative and militant. In other words, Christian hope should realize itself in a *creative and mili-*

---

9. Cf. Karl Rahner, "Kirche und Parusie Christi," *Schriften zur Theologie* (Einsiedeln: Benziger Verlag, 1965), 351.

tant eschatology. Our eschatological expectation does not look for the heavenly-earthly Jerusalem as that ready-made and existing, promised city of God. This heavenly city does not lie ahead of us as a distant and hidden goal, which only needs to be revealed. The eschatological City of God is *now* coming into existence, for our hopeful approach *builds* this city. We are workers building this future, and not just interpreters of this future. The power of God's promises for the future moves us to form this world into the eschatological city of God. The Council in the Constitution on the Church says, "*Renovatio mundi . . . in hoc saeculo reali quodam modo anticipatur.*" The Christian is a "co-worker" in bringing the promised universal era of peace and justice. The orthodoxy of a Christian's faith must constantly *make itself* true in the "orthopraxy" of his actions orientated toward the final future, because the promised *truth* is a truth which must be *made* (cf. John 3:21ff.).

The Christian eschatology therefore is not — despite its popularity among the existential theologians — a mere presential or actual eschatology, in which the passion for the future exhausts itself in a mere "making present" of eternity in the actual moment of personal decision. Nor is Christian eschatology a mere passive waiting, in which the world and its time-span appear as a waiting room, where the Christian lounges around in lackadaisical boredom until God opens the door of his office and allows the Christian to enter. Christian eschatology is, however, a productive and militant eschatology, which gradually realizes itself. Since Christian hope (is that very hope which) does not only eat its stew but must also brew its stew. An eschatological faith and an engagement in the world do not exclude one another. Because Paul's words "do not conform to the world" do not only mean that we should change ourselves, "but also that we should in conflict and creative expectation change the pattern of this world in which we believe, hope and love. The hope of the gospel has a polemical and a liberating relation to man's present and practical life and to the (social) conditions in which man leads his life."[10]

Fifth: A theology of the world which is guided by this creative-militant eschatology cannot unfold itself in the style and categories of the old theological cosmology. Moreover, it cannot discharge its task with the categories of a mere transcendental, personal, and existential theology because they are too individualistic and isolated. Since the theology of the world is not a mere theology of the cosmos or a mere transcendental theology of the human person and existence, but a theology of the emerging political and social order, this theology of the world must be

---

10. Cf. Jürgen Moltmann, *Theologie der Hoffnung,* 2d ed. (Munich: Ch. Kaiser Verlag, 1964), 304.

a *political theology*. An eschatologically orientated theology must place itself in communication with the prevailing political, social, and technical utopias and with the contemporary maturing promises of a universal peace and justice.

> The Christian salvation for which we hope is not only a personal salvation of one's soul or a mere rescuing of the individual from the evil world. Nor is it just a consolation for the personal conscience in temptation. It is *also* the achieving of an eschatological order of justice, the humanizing of man and the establishing of a universal peace. This "aspect" of our reconciliation with God has not been given sufficient prominence in the history of Christianity because Christians have no longer seen themselves in their true eschatological horizon, but have left the terrestrial-eschatological expectations to the fanatics and enthusiasts.[11]

In obeying its eschatological vocation Christianity should not establish itself as a ghetto society or become the ideological protective shell for the existing society. Rather it should become the liberating and critical force of this one society. Christianity should not establish itself as a "microsociety" beside the "great secular society." Any separation of Church and State leading to a ghetto or to a microsociety is fatal. The *terminus a quo* of the Christian mission should be the secular society. On this society must the "osmotic pressure" of the Christian hope be exerted. The various institutions of Christianity find their legitimation and also their criterion in their eschatological mission. Wherever these institutions serve Christianity's self-protection more than its venture forward (*nach vorn*), then the bastions of these institutions should be dismantled.

And finally: the Christian's militant hope is not simply a "militant optimism." Nor does it canonize man's own progress. His hope is rather a hope against every hope which we place in the manmade idols of our secular society. The Christian hope is not a cunning trick of man's reason in order to unravel the mysteries (*Entmysterialisierung*) of the future. Christian eschatology is not an omniscient ideology about the future, but a *theologia negativa* of the future. This poverty of knowledge is rather the very wealth of Christianity. What distinguishes the Christian and the secular ideologies of the future from one another is not that the Christians know *more*, but that they know *less* about the sought-after future of humanity and that they face up to this poverty of knowledge: "By faith Abraham obeyed when he was called to go out to a place which he was to receive as an inheritance; and he went out not knowing where he

---

11. Ibid., 303.

was to go" (cf. Heb. 11:8). Moreover, the Christian hope is aware of its own fatal perils; in short, it is aware of death. For in the face of death all shining promises fade away. This Christian hope is the anticipatory (proleptic) practice in dying. And even this aspect of hope should not be limited to an individualistic and worldless attitude. Christian hope is essentially directed to the world of our brother, since this hope fulfills itself in love for the other, for the least of our brothers. Only in this kenosis of love is death overcome. "We know that we have passed out of death into life, because we love the brethren" (cf. 1 John 3:14). The Christian hope enters into the passion of death in this kenosis of love to the least of our brothers. This is the imitation of Jesus: He did not live for himself, but for us. Hope is this living for "the other."

Chapter 2

The Church's Social Function in the Light of a "Political Theology"

The Problem of "Political Theology"

"Political theology" can mean several things and is therefore ambiguous. It also suffers from historical implications. Since space is lacking for a historical investigation of this concept, I beg the reader to understand it in the way I use it here and as I seek to explain it in the process. I happen to see it as a critical corrective to contemporary theology's tendency to concentrate on the private individual, and at the same time as a positive attempt to formulate the eschatological message in the circumstances of our present society.

The Function of Criticism within Theology

Let us briefly look at history before explaining the function of political theology as a critical corrective to contemporary theology.

The Historical Starting Point. The early Enlightenment in France was already aware of the fact that the unity and coordination of religion and society, of religious and social life, had collapsed. For the first time the Christian religion appeared as something special in its social environment. Its claim to universality was therefore recognized as conditioned by history. This problematic situation directly provoked the criticism of religion, first by the Enlightenment, later by Marxism. From the very start this criticism took the line which it still follows today: it criticizes religion as an ideology, in other words, it seeks to expose religion as a mere ideological superstructure based on a specific social practice and power structure. It seeks to expose the religious subject as suffering from a false consciousness, the consciousness of a society which is not, or not yet, genuinely aware of itself. A theology which tries to answer this criticism must of necessity grapple with the sociopolitical implications of its images and ideas. Briefly and frankly, I must say that classical metaphysical theology has failed to justify its position on this point. Its notions and categories assume in principle that there is no problem where the re-

26

lations between religion and society or between faith and social practice are concerned. As long as this assumption holds good, a purely metaphysical interpretation of religion may well be socially relevant as when, for example, medieval theology reached its peak. But when this unity collapses, such a metaphysical theology can no longer sit in judgment on the conflict between the Christian message and the sociopolitical reality, and it falls into a radical crisis.

The Modern Trend to Concentrate on the Private Individual. The present prevailing tendency in theology, with its transcendental, existential and personalist orientation, is fully aware of the problem created by the Enlightenment, and may even be said to have arisen as a reaction to it. But this reaction consisted mainly in treating the controversial social dimension of the Christian message implicitly or quite openly as not genuine or as secondary; in brief, it turned this message into a basically private concern and reduced the practice of the faith to a matter of mere individual decisions, unrelated to the world. This theology tries to solve the problem by eliminating it. It tries to overcome the Enlightenment without having passed through it. In the light of a religious consciousness, molded by this kind of theology, the sociopolitical reality has but an evanescent existence. The basic categories used in the interpretation of the message are preferably the intimate, the private, the apolitical. Charity, like all the phenomena of interpersonal relationships, is no doubt emphasized, but as something that is *a priori* and almost obviously private and stripped of political meaning, a mere I-and-thou relationship, an interpersonal encounter or a matter of neighborliness. The category of encounter dominates. The real religious expression is mutual contact, and the proper religious experience is the summum of subjective freedom or the shapeless, speechless, in between I-and-thou relationship. The present prevailing forms of transcendental, existential, and personalist theology seem to have one thing in common: concentration on what is private.

Demythologization and the Need to Reverse the Trend toward Concentration on the Private Individual. I would like to illustrate this trend by referring to the literary genre of the Christian message and its interpretation by modern theology. We know that the gospels do not intend to give us a biography of Jesus in the current sense of the word. The various accounts of Jesus do not belong to the genre of private biography but to that of public proclamation. The result of what is called Form Criticism has shown that the text of the gospels speaks at various levels. It seems to me unfortunate that these insights and discoveries of Form Criticism are at once interpreted in the terms of our theological existentialism and personalism. This turns our understanding of the proclamation *a priori* into the channels of the private and the intimate. The Word of proclamation is then understood as a personal self-communication of God to the private individual but not as a promise addressed to society. The hermeneutics of the existential interpretation of the New Testament remains imprisoned within the circle of a private I-and-thou relationship. We seem, therefore, to be in need of a new critical approach in order to reverse the basically individualistic tendencies in the very foundations of our theology.

The reversal of this "privatizing" tendency is the primary critical task of political theology. This "deprivatizing" seems to me in a certain sense as important as our demythologizing. It should at least accompany a legitimate demythologization, since this latter is constantly in danger of reducing God and salvation to a matter of private existence and of turning the eschatological message itself into a symbolic paraphrase of the metaphysical problem of man and the private situation in which he makes his decisions. But this deprives the promise of its conflicting and contradictory character with regard to the present state of reality and robs it of any power to influence society critically. This existentialist interpretation of the New Testament has a pronounced tendency toward individualism. It practices demythologization at the price of the myth of an existence detached from the world and soaked in private subjectivity.

The message of the New Testament clearly also has an element of legitimate individualization of the single person before God, which can be considered as a basic point of the message of the New Testament, particularly in its Pauline tradition. This *individualization* is not queried by the rejection of *individualism* because it is, on the contrary, precisely this tendency toward individualism which exposes theology to the danger of not touching the individual in the challenge of his existence. For this existence is today closely intertwined with the vicissitudes of society, and every existentialist and personalist theology that does not understand existence itself as a political problem in the broadest sense of the word remains today an abstraction insofar as the existential situation of the individual is concerned. Moreover, such an individualistic theology runs the risk of exposing the faith to modern sociopolitical ideologies in an uncritical and uncontrolled manner. Last, an ecclesiastical religion that sees itself in terms of such an individualistic theology assumes the character of "ineffective norms which are only binding insofar as they upset nobody and which still impress many in spite of being ineffective since they are incapable of producing anything else but their own repetitive reproduction."[1]

---

1. A. Gehlen, quoted in H. Schelsky, *Auf der Suche nach Wirklichkeit* (Düsseldorf, 1965), 271.

The Positive Task

Here we discover the positive task of political theology: it aims at re-assessing the relation between religion and society, between the Church and public society, between eschatological faith and social life, not in a precritical sense, in view of identifying these two realities, but in a post-critical sense, the sense of "second thoughts." As political, theology is forced to go in for these "second thoughts" if it wants to formulate the eschatological message in the condition and circumstances of modern society. Therefore, I want briefly to analyze the peculiarity of this situation and how to understand it as well as the peculiarity of the biblical message which determines this political theological reflection.

The Starting Point. The situation that gives rise to theological reflection today may be clarified by referring to a problem, already raised by the Enlightenment and no longer avoidable at least since Marx. The problem can briefly be posed as follows: According to Kant, he is enlightened who is free to make public use of his intelligence in all circumstances. To achieve such an enlightenment is therefore never a purely theoretical problem but in essence a political one, a problem of social life, that is, it is tied up with those sociopolitical assumptions which alone make enlightenment possible. Therefore, only he is enlightened who *at the same time* fights for the creation of those sociopolitical conditions on which the public use of one's intelligence depends.[2]

Where, then, the mind is determined on political freedom, and where, consequently, the theoretical transcendental reason appears *within* practical reason, and not the other way around, the mind must unavoidably go through a process of "deprivatization." And any "pure theory," however strained to the utmost, is only a falling back into a precritical consciousness. For now the critical claim of the subject can no longer be maintained as "purely theoretical." Here a new relationship operates between theory and practice, knowledge and morality, reflection and revolution, and this new relationship must also determine the theological consciousness if it does not want to fall back onto an earlier precritical stage of consciousness. Practical, and in the broadest sense of the word, political, reason must henceforth take part in every critical reflection of theology. Thus conceived in concrete terms, reason will have an increasing and concrete influence on the classical problem of the relation between faith and reason, and consequently on the problem of how to justify the faith. The so-called basic hermeneutic problem of theology is not really the question of the relation between systematic and historical theology, between

---

2. Cf. G. Picht, "Aufklärung und Offenbarung," in *Der Gott der Philosophen und die Wissenschaft der Neuzeit* (Stuttgart, 1966).

dogma and history, but that of theory and practice, of understanding the faith and social life. And so we have a brief description of the task of political reflection in theology as we discover it in the present situation. After all that has been said, it has nothing to do with a reactionary mixture of faith and politics, but it has everything to do with the unfolding of the sociopolitical potentiality of this faith.

The Biblical Tradition. Biblical tradition, too, forces us to have "second thoughts" about the relation between eschatological faith and social life. Why? Salvation, the object of Christian faith in hope, is not a private salvation. The proclamation of this salvation drove Jesus into a deadly conflict with the public authorities of his day. His cross does not stand in the exclusive privacy of the individual, nor in the sanctuary of a purely religious existence, but outside the threshold of sheltered privacy and the screen of the purely religious: it stands "outside," as the theology of the Epistle to the Hebrews formulated it. The veil of the Temple has definitely been torn. The scandal and the promise of this salvation are both equally public. This public aspect cannot be taken back, dissolved, or hushed up. It accompanies the message of salvation on its way through history. And in serving this message the Christian religion has been molded in the critical and liberating form of public responsibility.

All the authors of the New Testament are convinced that Christ is not a private person and the Church not a club. And so they have also reported on the encounter of Jesus Christ and his disciples with the political world and its representatives. No one understood this encounter more profoundly than John the Evangelist. In general, he sees the whole story of Jesus as a lawsuit which the world, represented by the Jews, brought or meant to bring against Jesus. This suit reaches the public judicial stage before Pilate, the representative of the Roman State and the wielder of political power.[3]

The whole composition of the passion narrative concentrates on this scene, but not when read with the eyes of Bultmann. The scene of Jesus before Pilate shows typical features.

From Eschatological to Political Theology. Political theology seeks to make contemporary theology once again aware of the suit pending between the eschatological message of Jesus and the reality of political society. It stresses that the salvation proclaimed by Jesus is permanently concerned with the world, not in the natural cosmological sense, but in

---

3. H. Schlier, *Besinnung auf das Neue Testament* (Freiburg, 1964), 193, more fully developed in the same author's *Die Zeit der Kirche* (Freiburg, 1956), 310.

the social and political sense, as the discerning and liberating element of this social world and its historical process. The eschatological promises of the biblical tradition — freedom, peace, justice, reconciliation — cannot be reduced to a private matter. They constantly force themselves into the sense of social responsibility. It is true that these promises never let themselves be simply identified with any given social situation, however much we try to determine and describe it from our point of view. The history of Christianity is only too well aware of that kind of direct identification of certain policies with the Christian promises. But in all these, that "eschatological proviso" has been lost which shows up the provisional condition of every social situation reached in the course of history, and I mean "provisional," not merely "arbitrary." For this "eschatological proviso" does not make us deny the social reality but creates a critical and dialectical attitude toward it. The promises toward which this proviso points are neither a distant void of religious expectation nor a mere regulative norm but a discerning and liberating imperative for our present. They are meant to be made operative and "embodied in truth" under the historical circumstances of the present, for their truth must be "done."[4]

The New Testament community knows that it has been called from the beginning to live the promise of the future in present conditions and thus to overcome the world. The orientation toward the promise of peace and justice changes every time our historical presence changes. It creates and forces us constantly into a fresh critical and liberating position with regard to the existing social environment in which we live. In a somewhat similar way, the parables of Jesus are parables of the Kingdom of God and *at the same time* parables that put us into a new critical relationship with the world that surrounds us. *Therefore, every eschatological theology must become a political theology in the sense of a theology of social criticism.*

This Is Not a New Science. This question of a political theology does not demand a new theological discipline with a separate sector of theological issues. This political theology rather means to lay bare in the first place a basic feature *within theological awareness at large.* It does not look at itself as excluded from the task of describing the content of faith and the working out of this in practice and from explaining the problem of life in faith within our world. It sees itself as the historical and concrete interpretation of theology as a whole. This life, this existence, is, as I have already stressed, a social and political theme in the broadest

---

4. For this requirement of a creative critical eschatology, see J. B. Metz, *The Word in History* (New York, 1966), 67–45.

sense of the word. Therefore, the process of rescuing it from the purely private sphere is in no sense a process of depersonalizing or vulgar collectivization. Its task is rather to see the situation of the faithful in the concrete and in all its aspects. Finally, it wants to put its reflection and its theological categories wholly at the service of the effort to find a language that is liberating and redeeming, so that "people will be shocked by it and yet be overcome by its power, the language of a new justice in truth, the language that proclaims the peace of God with men and the nearness of his Kingdom."[5]

The Church as the Institution of Free Social Criticism

Here we reach the second stage. In this theological perspective the Church appears not "by the side of" or "above" the social reality, but *within* it as an *institution of social criticism.*

Institutionalized Criticism

Because of its orientation toward the eschatological promises, faith develops a constantly fresh critical attitude toward its social environment. But can the individual faithful today shoulder this discerning freedom with regard to society in a compelling and effective manner? Does not precisely the *critical* aspect of this task of the faith bring up again the question of its institutionalization? Ideas can indeed persist and spread as long as they correspond to the needs of an age, a culture, or a social order, but not where they contain adverse criticism and must rely on the subjectivity of the individual.[6] Institution and institutionalization therefore emerge here not as a repression but as making a critical awareness *possible.* Must the faith not be institutionalized if it wants to shoulder this freedom of criticism with regard to present society? If so, does this question not point to a new understanding of the ecclesiastical institution? Does it not demand a Church which is *an institution of free criticism by faith?*

Two Objections

There are two objections to such a tentative definition of the Church.

(a) There is, first of all, the basic question whether an institution can be such an embodiment of criticism at all. Is "institutionalized criticism" not something like a square circle? Does every institution not imply an anticritical tendency? Is it not rather utopian to think of this postulated "institution of a second order" as not only the object, but also the embodiment of free criticism, as something which makes this criticism possible

---

5. D. Bonhoeffer, *Widerstand und Ergebung* (Munich, 1951), 207.
6. Cf A. Gehlen, *Anthropologische Forschung* (Hamburg, 1961), 76.

and ensures it? I can only counter this briefly with another question: Is the religious institution of the Church not specified precisely by the fact that it must be, and is, the bearer of such freedom of criticism? As an institution the Church itself lives under the "eschatological proviso." It does not exist for its own sake or for its own self-assertion, but for the historical affirmation of salvation for all. The hope it proclaims is not a hope for the Church but for the Kingdom of God. Thus, the institutional Church lives in the constant proclamation of its own provisional character. And it must translate this eschatological proviso institutionally into reality by being an institution of free criticism with regard to life in society with its absolutist and exclusive tendencies.

(b) Even if we can dispose of this objection in this way, we are faced with another critical question concerning the Church: What is the *historical and social ground* on which the Church can base this claim of free criticism? When was the Church such an institution of free criticism in actual fact? When was it not sheerly counterrevolutionary, embittered and mean in its relations with society? Has it not often failed to utter the criticism it should have made or uttered it far too late? Has it not constantly been exposed to the danger of being seen simply as an ideological superstructure on top of definite social situations and established power structures? Could it really still successfully wipe out this image? Is it not true that, particularly during the last centuries, the religious institution and critical reflection have each gone their own separate ways, so that today we have a theological reflection which is alien to the institution and an institution which is hostile to reflection? Where, then, do we find the historical and social basis for the claim that the Church has a critical institutional function with regard to society? The objection is valid. There is, so to speak, no single great social criticism made in our history — revolution, enlightenment, reason, or even love and freedom — which has not been disavowed at one time or another by historical Christianity and its institutions. Neither is there any point in trying to justify this by a kind of posthumous apologetics, even if it were possible; the only answer lies in a new "praxis," a new concrete attitude in the Church. Is there any hope of this coming about? I think there is, and what follows is based on this confidence.

The Liberating Critical Function of the Church in More Detail

In what does this liberating function of the Church exist with regard to our society and its historical process? What are the elements of that creative resistance which makes social progress real progress? Abandoning any method and any attempt at being complete, I would like to name only a few of these critical tasks.

The Defense of the Individual. Because of its eschatological proviso over against any abstract concept of progress and humanity, the Church protects the individual of the present moment from being used as material and means for the building up of a technological and totally rationalized future. It criticizes the attempt to see individuality merely as a function of a technologically controlled social process. No doubt, our social utopian ideals may well include a positive understanding of the individual. But does the individual count here only insofar as he is the first in opening up new social possibilities, and therefore insofar as he anticipates the social development in a revolutionary way? But what happens, then, to the poor and the oppressed, who are poor precisely because they can never be the first? Here the eschatological proviso of the Church with its institutional power of social criticism must protect an individuality which cannot be defined by its value for the progress of mankind.

Criticism of Totalitarianism. Another "critical" point seems to me to be that the Church must constantly use this liberating power of criticism with regard to all political systems; it must stress that history as a whole is subject to God's eschatological proviso. It must apply the truth that history as a whole can never be contained in a political idea in the narrow sense of the word, and therefore can never be limited to any particular political conduct. There is nothing within this world that can be designated as the subject of all history, and whenever a party, group, nation, or class sees itself as such a subject and consequently tries to dominate the whole process of history with its particular political interpretation, it must necessarily become totalitarian.[7]

Love as a Principle of Revolution. Finally, today more than ever, the Church must mobilize the potentiality of that Christian love that lies at the heart of its tradition. This love must not be confined to the interpersonal contact of I-and-thou. Nor should it be understood as a kind of philanthropy. It must be interpreted in its social dimension and made operative. This means that it must be understood as the unconditional commitment to justice, freedom, and peace *for others.* Understood in this way, love contains a power of social criticism, and this from two points of view.

On the one hand, this demands a committed criticism of *mere* force. It does not allow us to think in terms of "friend" and "enemy" because it commands us to love the enemy, and even to bring one's opponent within the sphere of one's own universal hope. The credibility and effectiveness of this criticism of pure violence will, to a large extent, depend on how

---

7. Cf. H. Lübbe, "Herrschaft und Planung," in *Die Frage nach dem Menschen* (Freiburg and Munich, 1966), 187–411.

far a Church, which puts itself forward as the Church of love, can avoid the appearance of being itself a religious power structure. After all, its mission is not to assert itself, but to affirm in actual history that salvation is there for all. It has, therefore, no power that precedes the power of its promises. That, in itself, is a preeminent criticism of power. It forces the Church into a passionate criticism of mere force, and it accuses the Church itself when, as so often in its history, the Church criticized the powerful of this world too meekly or too late, or when it hesitates to stand up for all threatened human beings without respect for persons, or when it does not passionately attack any form of contempt for human beings. This criticism of force does not mean that a Christian must withdraw from the wielding of any political power in every case. Such a basic withdrawal would be in itself an act against love of brother, for in his very faith and its tradition, the Christian has a principle by which to criticize this power.

Finally, Christian love as potential social criticism implies another aspect. When this love operates socially as the unconditional commitment to justice and freedom for others, it may in certain circumstances command something like *revolutionary force*. Where a social status quo is so full of injustice that it might equal that created by a revolutionary movement, then a revolution for the justice and freedom of "the least of the brethren" cannot be ruled out in the name of love. We should take Merleau-Ponty's objection that the Church has never yet supported a revolution more seriously since this objection is justified. Once again it becomes clear that the Church's function of social criticism always turns into a criticism of religion and of the Church itself. Both are only two faces of the same coin.

Consequences for the Self-Understanding of the Church

This function of social criticism is therefore bound to have a repercussion on the Church itself. In the long run it aims at *a new self-understanding of the Church* and at *a transformation of its institutional relationship with modern society*. I want to expand this somewhat. So far, what I have stated was based on the fact that not only the individual but the institutional Church as such is the bearer of this critical function toward society. This assumption rests on various grounds. One is the philosophy and sociology of modern critical awareness. It shows the uncertainties that beset the critical individual in his relations with this society and its anonymous structures. He demands an institutionalization of this criticism and so demands "institutions of a second order" which can carry and guarantee this freedom of criticism. Is the Church such an "institution of the second order"? The answer is "No" in its present form. I might go further and say "Not yet." How, and under what conditions can it become so? In answer, I would like to make a few observations in conclusion.

The New Language of the Church. We ask ourselves what in fact happens when the Church makes such a critical statement today? It has attempted to do so, as, for example, in some passages of the *Pastoral Constitution on the Church in the Modern World* and more clearly and definitely in the encyclical *Populorum progressio.* What happened? Here the institutional Church was forced to take note of, and assimilate, various *information* that did not simply spring from theological reflection in the ecclesiastical sense. Such critical statements, therefore, demand a new attitude toward nontheological information. Only when the Church accepts such information can it produce impulsive critical reactions that do not merely aim at self-assertion and self-reproduction. This kind of information will in the long run dislodge an uncritical monolithic self-awareness within the Church itself. This new source of information for ecclesiastical statements also requires a wholly *new way of expressing things, of speaking, in the Church.* Statements based on such information cannot be put forward in purely doctrinal terms. This demands that the Church have the courage to speak in contingent and hypothetical terms. What is required is an indication, which is neither lacking in force and sense of direction nor doctrinal and dogmatic. The present need of the Church to have to speak in a concrete critical way must therefore bring with it a kind of demythologization and deritualization of the Church's language and attitudes. The institutional Church now finds out that it must let itself be critically contradicted, that it cannot avoid a certain onesidedness and must therefore run the risk of saying something provisional. When it learns to speak in this way, it will also avoid burdening the social initiative of individual Christians with a doctrinal rigidity while removing a certain arbitrariness from such initiatives.

Public Criticism within the Church. Another point follows immediately on what has just been said: ecclesiastical criticism of society can only be credible and effective in the long run if it is based on growing public criticism within this Church. The reason is that without this public criticism no one would see to it that the institutional Church itself does not embody what it criticizes in others. Frankly, such public criticism within the Church so far has little to show for itself. I may, therefore, be allowed to name anew of the tasks this public criticism should undertake. One of them is critical opposition to every kind of ideological self-authorization assumed by ecclesiastical institutions; I mean opposition to any attempt to enforce quite definite sociopolitical and economic things through its own institutional measures. Another task is that of breaking down the uncontrolled domination within the Church of a prevalent social milieu — usually that of the small bourgeoisie — to the exclusion of others that are considered not to be normative or worthy of sharing in the public image of the Church. It should also be pointed out that the social images within the Church itself are historically conditioned and subject to change; since this change usually lags behind the social processes, it may be less easily recognized, but it nevertheless exists. A further aspect of public criticism is that it should oppose the Church when it is fighting on false battle fronts.

Very often the ingenuity spent on securing certain social positions would be more than adequate to change the situation. Finally, the institutional Church must also be seen to be effective in the exclusion of specific situations such as racism, individualistic nationalism, and any contempt of other human beings in whatever form. These examples may suffice. The courage to develop such public criticism in the Church will only grow with the confidence that there is a change in the institutional situation within the Church itself. But this confidence is perhaps one of the most important concrete manifestations of Church membership today.

The Importance of the Critical Attitude. A last observation: The sociocritical attitude of the Church cannot consist in the proclamation of one definite social order as the norm for our pluralistic society. It can only consist in that the Church operates its critical and liberating function in society and applies it to this society. The task of the Church is not a systematic social doctrine, but a *social criticism.* The Church, as a particular social institution, can only formulate its universal claim with regard to society without any ideology if it presents this claim as effective *criticism.* This basic critical attitude implies two important points. *First,* it will show that the Church, defined as a sociocritical institution, does not become a political ideology. No political party can have this criticism as its sole plank. Moreover, no political party can embrace in its political activity the whole scope of the Church's social criticism which covers the whole of history under God's eschatological proviso, otherwise it would drift into either romanticism or totalitarianism. *Second,* it is precisely this critical function of the Church that creates the basic possibility of *cooperation* with other non-Christian institutions and groups. The basis for such cooperation between Christians and non-Christians, between people and groups of the most varied ideological tendencies, can neither lie primarily in a positive determination of the social process nor in a definite notion of the substance of this free society of mankind in the future.

Within this positive perspective there will always be room for differences and pluralism. This pluralism within the positive perspective cannot be eliminated in our historical circumstances without substituting totalitarian manipulation for free realization. This cooperation should therefore be primarily an attitude of negative criticism and experience: the experience of threats to humanity, to freedom, justice, and peace. And we should not underrate this negative experience because here lies an elementary positive power of mediation. If, indeed, we may not immediately and directly agree on the positive meaning of freedom, peace, and justice, we all share a long-standing and common experience of what these things are *not*. And so this negative experience offers us an opportunity to unite, less, perhaps, in the positive planning of the freedom and justice we are seeking than in our critical opposition to the horror and terror of unfreedom and injustice. The solidarity bred by this experience, the possibility, therefore, of a common front of protest, must be understood and put into action. For the danger of "non-peace" remains too imminent. The irrational factors in our social and political conduct are only too clearly visible. We have not erased the possibility of collective obscurantism. The danger of "non-peace," unfreedom, and injustice is too great to allow us to remain indifferent in such matters for this indifference will inevitably lead to more criminal behavior in society.

Chapter 3

Christians and Jews after Auschwitz

Being a Meditation Also on the End of Bourgeois Religion

A Moral Awareness of Tradition

I am no expert in the field of Jewish-Christian ecumenism. And yet my readiness to voice an opinion on the question of Jewish-Christian relations after Auschwitz is motivated not least by the fact that I no longer really know — faced with the catastrophe of Auschwitz — what being an expert can possibly mean. So already that name has been uttered which cannot and should not be avoided when the relationship between Jews and Christians in this country — or in fact anywhere else — is being formulated and decided. It is a name which may not be avoided here, nor forgotten for an instant, precisely because it threatens already to become only a fact of history, as if it could be classified alongside other names in some preconceived and overarching history and thereby successfully delivered over to forgetfulness, or — amounting in the end to the same thing — to selective memorial celebrations: the name "Auschwitz," intended above all here as a symbol of the horror of that millionfold murder done to the Jewish people.

Auschwitz concerns us all. Indeed, what makes Auschwitz unfathomable is not only the executioners and their assistants, not only the apotheosis of evil revealed in these, and not only the silence of God. Unfathomable, and sometimes even more disturbing, is the silence of men: the silence of all those who looked on or looked away and thereby handed over this people in its peril of death to an unutterable loneliness. I say this not with contempt but with grief. Nor am I saying it in order to revive again the dubious notion of a collective guilt. I am making a plea here for what I would like to call a moral awareness of tradition. A moral awareness means that we can only mourn history and win from it standards for our own action when we neither deny the defeats present

39

within it nor gloss over its catastrophes. (Having an awareness of history and attempting to live out of this awareness means, above all, not evading history's disasters. It also means that there is at least one authority that we should never reject or despise — the authority of those who suffer.) If this applies anywhere, it applies, in our Christian and German history, to Auschwitz. The fate of the Jews must be remembered as a moral reality precisely because it threatens already to become a mere matter of history.

Auschwitz as End Point and Turning Point?

The question whether there will be a reformation and a radical conversion in the relations between Christians and Jews will ultimately be decided, at least in Germany, by the attitude we Christians adopt toward Auschwitz and the value it really has for ourselves. Will we actually allow it to be the end point, the disruption which it really was, the catastrophe of our history, out of which we can find a way only through a radical change of direction achieved via new standards of action? Or will we see it only as a monstrous accident within this history but not affecting history's course?

Let me clarify the personal meaning I attach to Auschwitz as end point and turning point for us Christians by recalling a dialogue I shared in. At the end of 1967 there was a roundtable discussion in Münster between the Czech philosopher Machoveč, Karl Rahner, and myself. Toward the end of the discussion, Machoveč recalled Adorno's saying: "After Auschwitz, there are no more poems" — a saying which is held everywhere today to be exaggerated and long since disproved — unjustly, to my mind, at least when applied to the Jews themselves. For were not Paul Celan, Thadeus Bowsky, and Nelly Sachs, among others — all born to make poetry as few others have been — destroyed by the sheer unalterability of that which took place at Auschwitz and the need for it somehow still to be uttered in language? In any case, Machoveč cited Adorno's saying and asked me if there could be for us Christians, after Auschwitz, any more prayers. I finally gave the answer which I would still give today: (We can pray *after* Auschwitz, because people prayed *in* Auschwitz.)

If this is taken as a comprehensive answer, it may seem as exaggerated a saying as Adorno's. Yet I do not consider it an exaggeration. We Christians can never again go back behind Auschwitz: to go beyond Auschwitz, if we see clearly, is impossible for us of ourselves. It is possible only together with the victims of Auschwitz. This, in my eyes, is the root of Jewish-Christian ecumenism. The turning point in relations

between Jews and Christians corresponds to the radical character of the
end point which befell us in Auschwitz. Only when we confront this end
point will we recognize what this "new" relationship between Jews and
Christians is, or at least could become.

To confront Auschwitz is in no way to comprehend it. Anyone wishing
to comprehend in this area will have comprehended nothing. As it gazes
toward us incomprehensibly out of our most recent history, it eludes our
every attempt at some kind of amicable reconciliation which would allow
us to dismiss it from our consciousness. The only thing "objective" about
Auschwitz are the victims, the mourners, and those who do penance.
Faced with Auschwitz, there can be no abstention, no inability to relate.
To attempt such a thing would be yet another case of secret complicity
with the unfathomed horror. Yet how are we Christians to come to terms
with Auschwitz? We will in any case forgo the temptation to interpret
the suffering of the Jewish people from our standpoint, in terms of saving
history. Under no circumstances is it our task to mystify this suffering!
We encounter in this suffering first of all only the riddle of our own
lack of feeling, the mystery of our own apathy, not, however, the traces
of God.

Faced with Auschwitz, I consider as blasphemy every Christian theodicy (i.e., every attempt at a so-called justification of God) and all language
about "meaning" when these are initiated outside this catastrophe or on
some level above it. Meaning, even divine meaning, can be invoked by us
only to the extent that such meaning was not also abandoned in Auschwitz itself. But this means that we Christians for our very own sakes
are from now on assigned to the victims of Auschwitz — assigned, in
fact, in an alliance belonging to the heart of *saving history*, provided the
word "history" in this Christian expression is to have a definite meaning
and not just serve as a screen for a triumphalist metaphysic of salvation which never learns from catastrophes nor finds in them a cause for
conversion since in its view such catastrophes of meaning do not in fact
exist at all.

This saving history alliance would have to mean, finally, the radical
end of every persecution of Jews by Christians. If any persecution were to
take place in the future, it could only be a persecution of both together,
of Jews and Christians — *as it was in the beginning*. It is well known
that the early persecutions of Christians were also persecutions of Jews.
Because both groups refused to recognize the Roman emperor as God,
thus calling in question the foundations of Rome's political religion, they
were together branded as atheists and haters of the human race and were
persecuted unto death.

The Jewish-Christian Dialogue
in Remembrance of Auschwitz

When these connections are seen, the question becomes obsolete as to whether Christians in their relations to Jews are now finally moving on from missionizing to dialogue. Dialogue itself seems, in fact, a weak and inappropriate description of this connection. For, after all, what does dialogue between Jews and Christians mean in remembrance of Auschwitz? It seems to me important to ask this question even though — or rather because — Christian-Jewish dialogue is booming at the present time and numerous organizations and institutions exist to support it.

1. Jewish-Christian dialogue in remembrance of Auschwitz means for us Christians first: It is not we who have the opening word, nor do we begin the dialogue. Victims are not offered a dialogue. We can only come into a dialogue when the victims themselves begin to speak. And then it is our primary duty as Christians to listen — *"for once to begin really listening"* — to what Jews are saying of themselves and about themselves. Am I mistaken in the impression I have that we Christians are already beginning in this dialogue to talk far too much about ourselves and our ideas regarding the Jewish people and their religion? That we are once again hastening to make comparisons, comparisons separated from concrete situations and memories and persons, dogmatic comparisons which may indeed be better disposed and more conciliatory than before but which remain equally naive because we are once more not listening closely? The end result is that the dialogue which never really achieved success is once more threatened with failure. And is not the reason for this that we are once again unable to see what is there, and prefer to speak about "Judaism" rather than to "the Jews"?

Have we really listened attentively during the last decades? Do we really know more today about the Jews and their religion? Have we become more attentive to the prophecy of their history of suffering? Or is the exploitation not beginning again, this time in a more sublime fashion because placed under the banner of friendliness toward the Jews? Is it not, for example, a kind of exploitation when we pick out fragments of texts from the Jewish tradition to serve as illustrations for our Christian preaching, or when we love to cite Hasidic stories without casting a single thought to the situation of suffering out of which they emerged and which is obviously an integral part of their truth?

2. No prepared patterns exist for this dialogue between Jews and Christians, patterns which could somehow be taken over from the familiar repertoire of inner-Christian ecumenism. Everything has to be measured by Auschwitz. This includes our Christian way of bringing into

play *the question of truth*. Ecumenism, we often hear, can never succeed if it evades the question of truth: it must therefore continually derive from this, its authentic direction. No one would deny this. But confronting the truth means first of all not avoiding the truth about Auschwitz, and ruthlessly unmasking the myths of self-exculpation and the mechanisms of trivialization which have been long since disseminated among Christians. This would be an ecumenical service to the one undivided truth! In general, Christians would be well advised, especially in dialogue with Jews, to show particular sensitivity in using the notion of truth. Too often, in fact, has truth — or rather what Christians all too triumphantly and uncompassionately portrayed as truth — been used as a weapon, an instrument of torture and persecution against Jews. Not to forget this for a moment belongs also to the respect for truth in the dialogue between Christians and Jews!

Something else has to be kept in mind, too: When we engage in this Christian-Jewish dialogue, we Christians should be more cautious about the titles we give ourselves and the sweeping comparisons we make. Faced with Auschwitz, who would dare to call our Christianity the "true" religion of the suffering, of the persecuted, of the dispersed? The caution and discretion I am recommending here, the theological principle of economy do not imply any kind of defeatism regarding the question of truth. They are rather expressions of mistrust in relation to any ecumenism separated from concrete situations and devoid of memory, that so-called purely doctrinal ecumenism. After Auschwitz, every theological "profundity" which is unrelated to people and their concrete situations must cease to exist. Such a theology would be the very essence of superficiality. With Auschwitz, the epoch of theological systems which are separate from people and their concrete situations has come to its irrevocable end. It is for this very reason that I am hesitant about all systematic comparisons of respective doctrines, however well intentioned and gentle in tone; hesitant also toward all attempts to establish "theological common ground." Everything about this is too precipitate for my liking. Besides, did this common ground not always exist? Why, then, was it unable to protect the Jews from the aggressive scorn of Christians? The problems must surely lie at a deeper level. We have to ask ourselves the question: Can our theology ever be the same again after Auschwitz?

3. There is yet another reason why the Jewish-Christian dialogue after Auschwitz eludes every stereotyped pattern of ecumenism. The Jewish partner in this sought-after new relationship would not only be the religious Jew, in the confessional sense of the term, but, in a universal sense, every Jew threatened by Auschwitz. Jean Amery expressed it thus, shortly before his death:

In the inferno [of Auschwitz] the differences now became more than ever tangible and burned themselves into our skin like the tattooed numbers with which they branded us. All "Arian" prisoners found themselves in the abyss elevated literally light-years above us, the Jews.... The Jew was the sacrificial animal. He had the chalice to drink — to its most bitter dregs. I drank of it. And this became my existence as Jew.

Christianity and Theology after Auschwitz

The sought-after ecumenism between Christians and Jews does not, of course, depend only on the readiness of Christians to begin at last to listen and to let Jews express themselves as Jews, which means as the Jewish people with their own history. This ecumenism contains also a fundamental theological problem regarding Christianity's own readiness, and the extent of this readiness, to recognize the messianic tradition of Judaism in its unsurpassed autonomy; as it were, in its enduring messianic dignity, without Christianity betraying or playing down the christological mystery it proclaims. Once again, this question is not to be handled abstractly but in remembrance of Auschwitz. Does not Auschwitz compel Christianity and Christian theology toward a radical inquiry into their own condition, a self-interrogation without which no new ecumenical evaluation of the Jewish religion and of Jewish history will be possible for Christians? I would like briefly to develop certain elements of this self-interrogation which seem important to me; these contain, moreover, just as many indications of constantly recurring and therefore quasi-endemic dangers within Christianity and its theology.

1. In the course of history, has not Christianity interpreted itself, in abstract contrast to Judaism, far too much as a purely "affirmative" religion, so to speak, as a theological "religion of conquerors" with an excess of answers and a corresponding lack of agonized questions? Was not the question of Job so repressed or played down within Christology that the image of the Son who suffers in relation to God and God's powerlessness in the world became all too adorned with the features of a conqueror? Does not the danger then arise of a christological reduction of the world's history of suffering? I want to illustrate what this means by a brief quotation from the German synodal document, *Our Hope:* "In the history of our church and of Christianity, have we not taken... Christ's suffering, in its hope-inducing power, and then separated it too much from the one history of suffering of humanity? In connecting the Christian idea of suffering exclusively with his cross and with ourselves as his disciples, have we not created gaps in our world, spaces filled with the un-

protected sufferings of others? Has not our attitude as Christians to this suffering often been one of unbelievable insensitivity and indifference" — as though we believed this suffering fell in some kind of purely profane sector, as though we could understand ourselves as the great conquerors in relation to it, as though this suffering had no atoning power, and as though our lives were not part of the burden placed upon it? How else, after all, is that history of suffering to be understood which Christians have prepared for the Jewish people over the centuries, or at least not protected them against? Did not our attitude in all that time manifest those typical marks of apathy and insensitivity which betray the conqueror?

2. Has not Christianity, precisely in comparison with the Jewish religion, concealed time and again its own messianic weakness? Does there not break through within Christianity, again and again, a dangerous triumphalism connected with saving history, something the Jews above all have had to suffer from in a special way? But is this the unavoidable consequence of Christian faith in the salvation definitively achieved in Christ? Or is it not true that Christians themselves still have something to await and to fear — not just for themselves, but rather for the world and for history as a whole? Must not Christians too lift up their heads in expectancy of the messianic Day of the Lord? This early Christian doctrine about expecting the messianic Day of the Lord — what level of intelligibility does it really have for Christian theologians? What meaning does it have — not only as a theme within Christian theology (one mostly dealt with in a perplexed or embarrassed way), but rather as a principle of theological knowledge? If this meaning were operative, or if Christians had rediscovered it in the light of Auschwitz, it would at once make clear that messianic trust is not identical with the euphoria about meaning often prevalent among Christians, something which makes them so unreceptive toward apocalyptic threats and perils within our history and allows them to react to the sufferings of others with the apathy of conquerors. And this meaning of the messianic Day of the Lord would make Christian theology perhaps more conscious of the extent to which the apocalyptic-messianic wisdom of Judaism is obstructed and repressed within Christianity. If the danger of Jewish messianism resides for me in the way it continually suspends all reconciliation from entering our history, the inverse danger in a Christian understanding of messianism seems to me to be the way it encloses the reconciliation given to us by Christ too much within the present, being only too prepared to hand out to its own form of Christianity a testimony of moral and political innocence.

Wherever Christianity victoriously conceals its own messianic weakness, its sensorium for dangers and downfalls diminishes to an ever greater degree. Theology loses its own awareness for historical disruptions and catastrophes. Has not our Christian faith in the salvation achieved for us by Christ been covertly reified to a kind of optimism about meaning, an optimism which is no longer really capable of perceiving radical disruptions and catastrophes within meaning? Does there not exist something like a typically Christian incapacity for dismay in the face of disasters? And does this not apply with particular intensity to the average Christian (and theological) attitude toward Auschwitz?

(3. Is there not manifest within the history of our Christianity a drastic deficit in regard to political resistance and a corresponding excess of political conformity?)This brings us, in fact, to what I see as the central point in the self-interrogation of Christians and of theology in remembrance of Auschwitz. In the earliest history of Christianity, as was already mentioned, Jews and Christians were persecuted together. The persecution of Christians ended, as we know, fairly soon; that of the Jews continued and increased immeasurably through the centuries. There are certainly numerous reasons for this dissimilar historical development in regard to Christians and Jews, and not all of them are to be used in criticism of Christianity.

Yet in making this observation, a question regarding our Christianity and its theology forces its way into my consciousness, a question that has long disturbed me and must surely affect every theology after Auschwitz: Has Christianity not allowed too strict an interiorization and individualization of that messianic salvation preached by Jesus? And was it not precisely this extreme interiorization and individualization of the messianic idea of salvation which placed Christianity — from its Pauline beginnings onward — at a continual advantage over against Judaism in coming to an arrangement with the political situation of the time and in functioning more or less without contradiction as an intermediary and reconciling force in regard to prevailing political powers? Has Christianity, perhaps for this reason only, been "in a better position"? Has the two-thousand-year-old history of Christianity contained less suffering, persecution, and dispersion than the history of the Jews for the very reason that with Christianity one could more easily "build a state"?

In a sense, Bismarck was on the right track when he said that with the Sermon on the Mount "no one can build a state." But has it then been an advantage, I mean a messianic advantage, that Christians have obviously always been more successful than Jews in knowing how to accommodate their understanding of salvation to the exigencies of political power by using this extreme individualization and interiorization? Should we not have expected to find in the history of Christianity many more conflicts with political power similar to the history of suffering and persecution of the Jewish people? Does not Christianity, in fact, manifest historically a shattering deficit in political resistance, and an extreme historical surplus of political accommodation and obedience? And finally, is it not the case that we Christians can recognize that concrete destiny which Jesus foretold for his disciples more clearly in the history of suffering undergone by the Jewish people than in the actual history of Christianity? As a Christian theologian, I do not wish to suppress this question, which disturbs me above all in the presence of Auschwitz.

This is the question that compelled me to project and work on a "political theology" with its program of deprivatization (directed more toward the synoptics than to Pauline traditions), to work against just these dangers of an extreme interiorization of Christian salvation and its attendant danger of Christianity's uncritical reconciliation with prevailing political powers. This theology argues that it is precisely the consistently nonpolitical interpretation of Christianity, and the nondialectical interiorizing and individualizing of its doctrines, that have continually led to Christianity taking on an uncritical, as it were, postfactum political form. But the Christianity of discipleship must never be politicized postfactum — through the copying or imitation of political patterns of action and power constellations already present elsewhere. Christianity is in its very being, as messianic praxis of discipleship, political. It is mystical and political at the same time, and it leads us into a responsibility, not only for what we do or fail to do but also for what we allow to happen to others in our presence, before our eyes.

4. Does not Christianity conceal too much the *practical core* of its message? Time and again we hear it said that Judaism is primarily oriented toward praxis and less concerned with doctrinal unity, whereas Christianity is said to be primarily a doctrine of faith, and this difference is held to create considerable difficulty for Jewish-Christian ecumenism. Yet Christianity itself is not in the first instance a doctrine to be preserved in maximum "purity," but a praxis to be lived more radically! This messianic praxis of discipleship, conversion, love, and suffering does not become a part of Christian faith postfactum, but is an authentic expression of this faith. Ultimately, it is of the very essence of the Christian faith to be believed in such a way that it is never just believed, but rather — in the messianic praxis of discipleship — enacted. There does, of course, exist a Christianity whose faith is only believed, a superstructure Christianity serving our own interests — such a Christianity is bourgeois religion. This kind of Christianity does not live discipleship but only believes in discipleship and, under the cover of merely believed-in discipleship, goes its own way. It does not practice compassion, but only believes in compassion and, under the screen of this merely

believed-in compassion, cultivates that apathy which allowed us Christians to continue our untroubled believing and praying with our backs to Auschwitz — allowed us, in a phrase from Bonhoeffer, to go on singing Gregorian chant during the persecution of the Jews without at the same time feeling the need to cry out in their behalf.

It is here, in this degeneration of messianic religion to a purely bourgeois religion, that I see one of the central roots within contemporary Christianity for our failure in the Jewish question. Ultimately, it is the reason why we Christians, as a whole, have remained incapable of real mourning and true penance, the reason also why our churches have not resisted our society's massive repression of guilt in these postwar years.

Presumably, there are still other Christian and theological questions posed to us in remembrance of Auschwitz, questions which would open a way to an ecumenism between Christians and Jews. We would certainly have to uncover the individual roots of anti-Semitism within Christianity itself, in its doctrine and praxis. A continual and significant part of this is that relationship of "substitution within salvation history," through which Christians saw themselves displacing the Jews and which led to the Jews never being really accepted either as partners or as enemies — even enemies have a countenance! Rather, they were reified into an obsolete presupposition of saving history. However, this specific inner Christian research cannot be undertaken here; it would go far beyond the limits of this paper. I must also rule out here any investigation of the roots of anti-Semitism in those German philosophies of the nineteenth century which in their turn have lastingly marked the world of theological ideas and categories in our own century.

(What Christian theologians can *do* for the murdered of Auschwitz and thereby for a true Christian-Jewish ecumenism is, in every case, this: Never again to do theology in such a way that its construction remains unaffected, or could remain unaffected, by Auschwitz. In this sense, I make available to my students an apparently very simple but, in fact, extremely demanding criterion for valuating the theological scene: Ask yourselves if the theology you are learning is such that it could remain unchanged before and after Auschwitz. If this is the case, be on your guard!)

Revisions

The question of reaching an ecumenism between Christians and Jews, in which the Jews would not be compelled to deny their own identity, will be decided ultimately by the following factor: Will this ecumenical development succeed within the church and within society? Theological work for reconciliation remains nothing more than a surface phenomenon when it fails to take root in church and society, which means touching the soul of the people. Whether this ecumenism successfully takes root, and the manner of its success, depends once again on the way our churches, as official institutions and at the grassroots level, relate to Auschwitz.

What is, in fact, happening in our churches? Do not the "Weeks of Christian-Jewish Fellowship" threaten gradually to become a farce? Are they not a witness to isolation far more than to fellowship? Which of us are really concerning ourselves about the newly emerging fears of persecution among the Jews in our country? The Catholic Church in West Germany in its synodal decree, *Our Hope*, declared its readiness for a new relationship with the Jewish people and recognized its own special task and mission. Both the history behind the preparation of this section of the synod's text and its finally accepted form could show how tendencies to hush up and exonerate had a powerful impact. Nevertheless, if we would only take this document really seriously even in this final version! "In that time of national socialism, despite the exemplary witness of individual persons and groups, we still remained as a whole a church community which lived its life with our backs turned to the fate of this persecuted Jewish people; we let our gaze be fixed too much on the threat to our own institutions and remained silent in the face of the crimes perpetrated on the Jews and on Judaism."

Yet, in the meantime, has not a massive forgetfulness long since taken over? The dead of Auschwitz should have brought upon us a total transformation; nothing should have been allowed to remain as it was, neither among our people nor in our churches. Above all, not in the churches. They, at least, should necessarily have perceived the spiritual catastrophe signified by Auschwitz, one which left neither our people nor our churches undamaged. Yet, what has happened to us as Christians and as citizens in this land? Not just the fact that everything happened as if Auschwitz had been, after all, only an operational accident, however deplorable a one. Indications are already appearing that we are once more beginning to seek the causes for the Auschwitz horror, not only among the murderers and persecutors, but also among the victims and persecuted themselves. How long, then, are we to wear these penitential garments? This is a question asked above all by those who have probably never had them on. Has anyone had the idea of asking the victims themselves how long we have to drag out our penance and whether something like a general "limitation of liability" does not apply here? The desire to limit liability in this area is to my mind less the expression of a will to forgiveness from Christian motives (and indeed *we* have here hardly anything to forgive!) than it is the attempt of our society and of our Christianity(!) to decree for itself — at last — acquittal and, poised over the abyss of horror, to get the whole thing — at last — "over with."

Faced with this situation, one thing is clear: The basis for a new relationship between Christians and Jews in remembrance of Auschwitz must not remain restricted to the creation of a diffuse sense of reconciliation nor to a Christian friendliness toward Jews which is as cheap as it is ineffective (and is itself, in fact, not seldom the sign of an unfinished hostility to Jews). What must be aimed at is a concrete and fundamental revision of our consciousness.

To take one example: This new dialogical relationship we are seeking, if it is truly to succeed, must not become a dialogue of theological experts and church specialists. This ecumenism must take root in the people as a whole, in the pedagogy of everyday life, in Sunday preaching, in church communities, families, schools, and other grassroots institutions. Everyone knows that new traditions are not established in advanced seminars nor in occasional solemn celebrations. They will only emerge if they touch the souls of men through a tenacious process of formation, when they become the very environment of the soul. But what is actually happening here in our churches and schools? Not least in our churches and schools in the rural areas which are held to be so "Christian"? Certainly anti-Semitism in rural areas has varied causes; yet not the least of these are related to religious education. In my own rural area, in a typically Catholic milieu, "the Jews" remained even after the war a faceless reality, a vague stereotype; representations for "the Jews" were taken mostly from Oberammergau.

Some historians hold the view that the German people in the Nazi era were not, in fact, essentially more anti-Semitic than several other European peoples. Personally, I doubt this, but if it were true, it would raise an even more monstrous possibility, something already put forward years ago by one of these historians: Might the Germans have drawn the ultimate consequences of anti-Semitism, namely the extermination of the Jews, only because they were commanded to; that is, out of sheer dependence on authority? Whatever the individual connection may have been, there is manifest here what has often enough been established as a "typically German danger." And this is the reason why the question being dealt with here demands the highest priority being given by both society and the churches to an energetic educational campaign supporting critical obedience and critical solidarity, and against the evasion of conflict and the practice of successful conformism, opportunism, and fellow-traveling.

In this context I want to quote, without pursuing her argument further, the thoughts of a young Jewish woman, who worked as a teacher in West Germany, regarding the Week of Fellowship:

> There are two expressions I learned in the school without having the least idea of their significance. One of them is "in its juridical form," and the other is "legal uncertainty." Every event in the school, and I assume in all other institutions, has to be confirmed in its juridical form, even when this leads to senseless behavior.... Wherever I look, I see only exemplary democrats who, according to the letter and without any reason or emotion, observe laws and ordinances, instructions, directions, guiding lines and decrees. The few who protest against this and display some individualism and civil courage are systematically intimidated and cowed.... That is the reason why I do not fraternize with the Germans, why I reject the Week of Fellowship, and why my soul boils over at the empty babble about our dear Jewish brethren; the same people who today speak eloquently of tolerance would once again function as machines which had been presented with a new and different program!

At the beginning, I mentioned that Auschwitz can only be remembered by us as a moral reality, never purely historically. This moral remembrance of the persecution of the Jews touches finally also on the relationship of people in this country to the *State* of Israel. Indeed, *we* have no choice in this matter (and I stand by this against my left-wing friends). *We* must at all events be the last people to now accuse the Jews of an exaggerated need for security after they were brought in the most recent history of our country to the edge of total annihilation; and we must be the first to trust the protestations of the Jews that they are defending their state, not from reasons of Zionist imperialism but as a "house against death," as a last place of refuge of a people persecuted through the centuries.

Ecumenism in a Messianic Perspective

The ecumenism between Jews and Christians in remembrance of Auschwitz, which I have been discussing here, does not lead at all to the outskirts of inner Christian ecumenism, but rather to its center. It is my profound conviction that ultimately ecumenism among Christians will only make progress at all, and certainly will only come to a good conclusion, when it recovers the biblical-messianic dimensions of ecumenism in general. This means it must learn to know and recognize the forgotten and suppressed partner of its own beginnings, the Jewish people and their messianic religion. It is in this sense that I understand Karl Barth's warning in his 1966 "Ecumenical Testament": "We do not wish to forget that there is ultimately only one really central ecumenical question: This is our relationship to Judaism." As Christians, we will only come together among ourselves when we achieve together a new relationship to the Jewish people and to its religion; not avoiding Auschwitz, but as that particular form of Christianity which, after Auschwitz, is alone permitted to us and indeed demanded of us. For, I repeat: We Christians can never again go back behind Auschwitz. To go beyond Auschwitz is, if we see clearly, impossible for us of ourselves; it is possible only together with the victims of Auschwitz.

And so we could arrive one day, although I suggest this cautiously, at a kind of *coalition of messianic trust* between Jews and Christians in opposition to the apotheosis of banality and hatred present in our world. Indeed, the remembrance of Auschwitz should sharpen all our senses for present-day processes of extermination in countries in which on the surface "law and order" reigns as it did once in Nazi Germany.

Chapter 4

Bread of Survival

*The Lord's Supper of Christians as Anticipatory Sign
of an Anthropological Revolution*

The Crisis of Survival or the Social Apocalypse
of a Dominating Way of Life

What does man live on? Whose bread does he eat? Which food nourishes his life? Nietzsche: "I am Zarathustra, the godless; I keep cooking for myself in my pot every kind of chance. And only when it is well cooked through, do I welcome it as my food. And verily, many a chance came to me domineeringly; yet still more domineeringly did my will speak to it — and at once it lay there imploringly on its knees." Bread of domination over chance, food of power and subjugation of the play of nature: Is this the bread upon which we live? Is that the food that nourishes us? But what then does Nietzsche's "Grace at meals" have to do with the pervasive question of survival today? Perhaps a lot, perhaps everything; it leads us, in my view, into the center of what is called our crisis of survival.

This crisis of survival, which is being discussed today as the ecological question, is, in fact, not least dependent on the problem of the over-burdening and overexploitation of the nature surrounding us. For if we want to achieve new ways of relating to nature and to practice eco-logical wisdom, we cannot simply begin in pretended innocence with "nature" alone. Nature itself cannot become the principle of a new way of action without some kind of mediation, without some permeation of nature through society and anthropology. Otherwise we would be driven only too easily, as our most recent German history leads us to fear, into typically fascistic attitudes (of "blood and soil"). We have to begin with the history human beings have with nature. But this is a history of domination, a history of subjugation.

At the beginning of what we call "the Modern Age," the limits of which we are now reaching with ever-increasing clarity, there unfolds — embryonically and overlaid with many religious and cultural symbols — this anthropology of domination. In it man understands himself as a

53

dominating, subjugating individual over against nature; his knowledge becomes, above all, knowledge via domination, and his praxis is one of exerting power over nature. In this dominating subjugation, in this activity of exploitation and reification, in this seizing power over nature, man's identity is formed. Man is by subjugating. All nondominating human virtues such as gratitude and friendliness, the capacity for suffering and sympathy, grief and tenderness, recede into the background. They are deprived of social and cultural power or, at best, in a treacherous "division of labor" they are entrusted to women, who are deprived of power anyway in this dominating male culture. These nondominating attitudes become undervalued also as unique kinds of knowledge. What dominates is knowledge as subjugation: knowing as "grasping," as "appropriating," as a kind of taking possession. Other forms of sensitive-intuitive access to reality, such as through the eyes and their gaze, are forced aside into the realm of the private and the irrational.

In the meantime, this principle of subjugation has long since permeated the psychic foundations of our total sociocultural life. It has become the secret regulating principle of all interpersonal relationships; the psychosocial pathologies of our times provide a surfeit of illustrative material on this. In this sense, we could and should speak, not only — and not even primarily — of a poisoning through unrestricted technical exploitation of the outer nature surrounding man, but also of a poisoning of the inner nature of man himself. (An identity thus formed through the principles of domination and subjugation makes the individual profoundly disconnected and, in the strict sense of the term, egoistic. It makes the human being incapable of seeing himself and judging himself through the eyes of his victims.)

These marks of a dominating anthropology may have long since escaped us, since the drive to subjugation which belongs to this form of anthropological identity shifted its focus very early on outwards — against foreign minorities, foreign races, and foreign cultures. The European history of colonization has its roots therein, and the fact that the history of Christian missions accompanied this all too closely, arching, as it were, over this history of subjugation, may serve as an illustration of the pervasive way the mechanism of subjugation has also penetrated our church life and religious life. (In a kind of objective cynicism, we speak frequently today of so-called underdeveloped peoples. When we look more closely, it is often a question of peoples whose cultures we have subjugated, devastated, and exploited.)

This anthropological model of man as an essentially dominating kind of being is intrinsic to our European scientific-technological civilization. The inner tendency of natural science and large-scale technology will not be anthropologically neutralized by the fact that technology in both the major social systems, in Western bourgeois capitalism as well as in the hitherto-existing forms of socialism, is employed as a supposedly neutral instrument. On the contrary, it is precisely this societal concealment which makes possible the most tenacious and all-pervasive efficacy of the anthropological principle of subjugation intrinsic to it. It is hard to doubt, for example, that bourgeois identity is formed in its very essence by such a principle. And where would the struggle for what could be called a new, postbourgeois human being be so successful that we would not discover again in this human being those same features of domination, and could, therefore, gaze on his image without fear?

This necessarily brief analysis is not, however, accompanied by the expectation of a gradual euthanasia of natural science and large-scale technology in general. It is rather a question of using these more critically and with greater caution; above all, of not exposing ourselves (or at least much less than before) to the anonymous pressure of the anthropology of domination intrinsic to them. The basic issue is that we should not let the concept of "life" be secretly presented and defined for us from that direction. And the anthropological revolution this entails goes to the very roots; its dimensions are given by the way in which the model of domination has long since permeated everything; this revolution affects the whole societal construction of our reality, of our political and economic systems. This fact is causing the massive helplessness and fear we see today; apathy or resignation are already eating away at the soul. Overnight, our dominating dreams of progress have collapsed into contagious fears for survival.

Yet the paradox is this: When life aims only at survival, even that success will soon be denied it. We will, in fact, only survive, only save our lives, when we understand what life is about. And so I repeat the question we began with: "What does man live on? Whose bread does he eat? Which food nourishes his life?" What is this deprivation which is depriving us of life itself, making it in any case weaker, almost invisible?

Living on the "Bread of Life"

At the center of their eucharistic community, Christians recall the passion, death, and resurrection of him who — in the language of John's gospel — said of himself, "I am the bread of life" (6:35, 48). And in the same gospel, we hear also that word concerning the food from which this life is once more secretly nourished: "My food is to do the will of him who sent me" (4:34). Nietzsche formulated it very differently.

Living on this "bread of life" is not without its danger, once we have grown all too used to that other nourishment provided for us by the anthropology of domination, of the will to power and to subjugation. A serious changeover to this "bread of life" can make us at first downright sick, at least in the eyes of those obsessed with normality. But this will be a "sickness unto life" — to that life without which life itself perhaps will soon no longer survive. This bread can become for us the nourishment and sacrament of life, precisely because in the midst of our life of domination it gives visible shape to death, suffering, love, fear, and grief, and gives us power to take these into ourselves. Of course, only a few aspects of all this can be developed here.

(1. This eucharistic "bread of life" makes us receptive to death. It draws death, as it were, back into life, allows death a renewed place in our life, so that this life might indeed become something other than pure survival. It is, in fact, not death itself which alienates us from ourselves and snatches life from us: it is, instead, the suppression of death, the flight from death. This suppression of death has made us into those dominating beings bent on subjugation who today are everywhere encountering the limits of their survival.)

For what is the real background to this process of subjugation, exploitation, and reification of nature that marks our history of progress? Does not man experience in this nature — a nature that confronts him as something alien and indifferent, and whose waves will roll over him tomorrow as they do the grains of sand at the ocean — his own death and his own downfall? And is not, therefore, the aggressive, unrestrained, total subjection of this nature ultimately the attempt made by man as dominator to remove death from the world? In this sense, is not our scientific-technological civilization with its drive toward the total subjugation of nature a single gigantomachy of the repression of death? Is not the infinite path of our progress, in essence, a way of escape, a way to flee death? And whither does it lead us? Into life? The repression of death has made us into insatiable subjugators. Yet, in the meantime, have we not long since become subjected to our own principle of subjugation, that principle of domination in which all life rich in relationships is being increasingly extinguished? Subjected to that power of domination which can only repress death by producing in its turn ever new dead relationships, so that the question of a life before death is becoming increasingly reduced to the question of naked survival?

2. The eucharistic "bread of life" strengthens us in our receptivity toward suffering and those who suffer. A life nourished by this bread allows suffering to exist in a new way, makes the sufferings of others visible, so as to transform them into our own. Here again it is not suffering as such which alienates us from ourselves and robs us of life — it is rather

the repression and reification of suffering, the pure flight from suffering. (Only when people themselves remain capable of suffering do they refrain from forcing suffering arbitrarily upon others, and are able and ready in their own way to share in the sufferings of others and become active in the liberation struggles of the tortured and the exploited. The same Nietzsche who forces into submission all sufferings afflicting him and cooks them into the food of his domineering will becomes the great enemy of compassion toward the sufferings of others. The culture of the subjugators is one of apathy and disconnectedness from others. Their support is given to the suffering only when this enables them to come to power once more and thereby confirm their unbroken domination.

A eucharistic community nourished by the "bread of life" draws the capacity for suffering back into the life of apathy. It attempts to give this ability to suffer a new power to exist and to endure within a rapacious society which, in its revealing way, often simply covers up its suffering cosmetically, deadens it with painkillers, or seeks to organize it away through paternalistic bureaucracies designed to make suffering socially invisible. The question, of course, is: Do we Christians really let ourselves be nourished by the "bread of life" in a life-giving direction, toward the capacity for suffering? Or do we simply believe in compassion and remain under the cloak of a mere belief in compassion fixed within the apathy which accompanies life as domination? Does the sacrament of this bread really make the invisible sufferings of the brethren visible to us, so that through sharing in their suffering we may pass over from death into life? Does it give us back that power which we have lost under the domination of the principle of subjugation, that power which lets us look at ourselves and judge ourselves with the eyes of our own victims?

What kind of receptivity, for example, do we have toward the fact that our Christianity is itself generating profound and anguishing social oppositions, which are also class oppositions between the rich and poor churches? Through such oppositions Christians, as long as they remain in their apathy, are literally bringing death each day to those other Christians who are their table companions at the eucharistic meal? In this context, what has been called "The Text on Hope" of the Catholic synod in West Germany puts it this way:

> In our service to the one church, we cannot allow it to happen that church life in the Western world should more and more give the impression of a religion of prosperity and satiety, whereas in other parts of the world it looks like a common religion of the unfortunate, whose lack of bread literally excludes them from our Eucharistic table fellowship. Otherwise, there emerges before the

gaze of the world the scandal of a church combining within itself the unfortunate and the spectators of misfortune, the many sufferers and the many Pilates, and calling this whole reality the one table fellowship of believers, the one People of God.

Are we this scandal or are we not? Is our Eucharist a cult of life or of apathy?

3. The eucharistic "bread of life" nourishes us toward love. It wants to bring love back into the life of domination, and exorcize that interiorized capitalism, that attitude of grasping and struggling for advantage. "Those who possess their life will lose it, and those who hold it worthless will gain it." We have every reason, confronted by this shocking saying, to feel fear — at least if we had decided just to believe in love, but under the cloak of mere belief to remain the same dominating egoists, men of subjugation and power who have long since subjected everything they call "love" to this principle of domination and who now practice this "love" as subordinational and paternalistic love within marriage, family, and society. Yet to repeat again: It is not, in fact, the kind of love that forgets its own advantage and possessions which alienates us from ourselves and robs us of life, but rather the very repression of this love, the flight from love, and that prohibition of love secretly dominating our modern societies.

Where Christians truly nourish themselves from the food of this love, their eucharistic community will become the symbol and the provocation for a new and unprecedented praxis of sharing among themselves and with others. And much toward which this love drives us may appear as a form of betrayal, a betrayal of our existing prosperity and property, a betrayal of our bourgeois class and of the ingrained ideals of our life of domination.

4. The "bread of life" becomes for us finally the food of mourning and of fear. The life to which this bread nourishes us does not want to make us invulnerable and unassailable. The eucharistic prayers refuse, therefore, to become for us an imaginary ladder allowing us to climb swiftly away beyond our own fears and our own grief. Accordingly, the eucharistic bread wants to give us strength, not for the hasty suppression of fear and mourning, nor for a swift recovery from these, but rather in order to let them exist. And once again: It is not the mourning and fear which alienate us from ourselves and rob us of life, but rather the repression of fear and grief, the flight from mourning. That famous saying about the "inability to mourn" is not just a statement within social pathology about the German mentality in the postwar years; it is a fundamental statement about every form of humanity which builds up its own identity through subjugation and domination. This subjugating form of humanity

stands under a downright prohibition of mourning and melancholy; it is accompanied by the denunciation of grief as an unbecoming, helpless sentimentality. These prohibitions of mourning and melancholy in East and West — nowhere decreed but everywhere effective — speak indeed a language of their own. And this kind of humanity stands under the prohibition of fear; for its ruling principle of domination and power defines freedom in complete opposition to experiences such as grief and fear, which possess value neither for domination nor for exchange. This suppressed fear, however, throws people back again upon the supposedly unassailable life of domination and robs them in the end of all fantasy regarding their search for life, and what deserves the name of life.

What does man live on? Whose bread does he eat? Which food nourishes his life? Why has he lost hold of life so that he is fearful about his very survival? I make bold to say: The eucharistic "bread of life" provokes those who are nourished by it, and who make it their life's food, to begin a kind of "anthropological revolution." This would be what we could call the specifically Christian way of dealing with the crisis of survival prevailing today, a crisis which is not primarily a cosmological problem but an anthropological and political one. I cannot see how, without such a revolution, a way out of this crisis of survival that does not involve some kind of catastrophe is possible at all. If we Christians do not want to become mere helpers in the survival strategy of the already rich and powerful peoples, a strategy that will in every way increase the burden of the poor and long-exploited human beings, we have to risk this anthropological revolution and prepare a rebellion against the catastrophe "which consists in the fact that everything keeps going on as before" (W. Benjamin).

Anthropological Revolution

That anthropological revolution which is now to be described in an extremely abbreviated form is without analogy in the modern history of revolution. Perhaps we could describe it as a revolutionary formation process for a new subjectivity. Yet such an expression is open to misunderstanding. In any case, it is a process of liberation we are discussing. And the theology aiming at this process of liberation would be that "theology of liberation" to which we are challenged and which is required of us in our situation, so that we might not betray or leave in the lurch — or even denounce as downright un-Christian — that other theology of liberation in the countries on the shadow side of this earth.

The process of liberation generated by the anthropological revolution differs, both in its inner content and in its outer direction, from the ideas of social revolution current among us. For this revolution is not, in fact, concerned with liberating us from our poverty and misery, but rather from our wealth and our totally excessive prosperity. It is not a liberation from what we lack, but from our consumerism in which we are ultimately consuming our very selves. It is not a liberation from our state of oppression, but from the untransformed praxis of our own wishes and desires. It is not a liberation from our powerlessness, but from our own form of predominance. It frees us, not from the state of being dominated but from that of dominating; not from our sufferings but from our apathy; not from our guilt but from our innocence, or rather from that delusion of innocence which the life of domination has long since spread out through our souls This revolution seeks to bring to power precisely the nondominating virtues and, in fact, in this context to liberate our society also from a culture dominated totally by males. It is not surprising that for this kind of revolution no basis exists among the masses, everything remains extremely nebulous. The bearers of this revolution are scarcely identifiable and its formulation in political terms remains vague. I will deal with these issues a little later on.

First, however, the contradiction has to be explained between the anthropological revolution and our prevailing ideas about what revolutions are. Marx once described them as the locomotive of world history. Walter Benjamin has made the following critically reflective commentary on that statement: "Perhaps the opposite is really the case. Perhaps revolutions happen when the human race, riding within this train, pulls the emergency brake." This would be revolution, not as a dramatically accelerated progress, nor as aggressively heightened evolution, but rather as a rebellion against the fact that "everything keeps going on as before." This would be revolution as interruption, which seems to me exactly the direction aimed at by the anthropological revolution. We Christians possess a central word for this: conversion, the change of hearts. Such a conversion, when it becomes the expression of a *life* of faith and not just of a *belief in* faith, goes through people like a shock, reaching deep down into the direction their lives are taking, into their established systems of needs and desires. It damages and disrupts our immediate self-interest and aims at a fundamental reorganization of our habitual way of life. The food that nourishes this revolutionary conversion is the "bread of life."

This anthropological revolution could be called our Christian reaction to the so-called crisis of survival. It is our attempt to achieve a new relationship to ourselves, to our natural and social environment, which is not one of domination and exploitation. It is our intrinsic contribution to ecology, and its inspiration comes from the heart of our eucharistic community. But this revolution, this struggle against ourselves, against our dominating-exploiting identity is simultaneously and indivisibly the fundamental praxis of our solidarity with the poor and exploited peoples of this earth. Their poverty and our wealth, their powerlessness and our predominance, are bound together in a relationship of dependency. Hence, in the same way, the will to freedom of these peoples corresponds in our own situation to our struggle with ourselves, the struggle against the ingrained ideals of "always having more," against the total penetration of our entire biosphere by domination and competition. Only where this social dialectic proper to the ecological question is kept in view will the struggle for survival waged on its behalf among us today avoid becoming a last attempt to save ourselves by burdening those who are already weak and oppressed.

This revolution may well be branded by some as inadequate, and by others as transparent betrayal. Yet no one should underestimate its political and social significance. For every revolution conceived only in social and economic terms, however purposeful and strategically intelligent its beginnings may be among the oppressed and injured masses, will fail if, in its development, it does not risk this anthropological revolution. It will fail if it considers such a thing already attained or even rendered obsolete by the social revolution it has struggled for or is struggling toward. What this will lead to will be only a rearrangement and a new division of those relationships of subjugation and dependency. It will not become the power overcoming this life of domination, but rather the power accomplishing it. Nietzsche would then remain still the stronger force within Marx!

But how and where can this anthropological revolution and the political culture envisaged by it take on concrete form? Who can bring it into being?

Basic Communities as Bearers of the Anthropological Revolution

The dimensions of the crisis of survival in contemporary society are increasingly leading to a situation in which moral and pedagogical principles are being reinstated within politics, with politics and morality being thereby reunited in a new way. The meaning of life and the quality of life, the revision of priorities in life, the acceptance of limits within life, renunciation and ascesis, a change of hearts — all these are maxims of survival we hear today, and these and similar demands are emerging more and more within today's political vocabulary. Up till now they have remained rather diffuse, occasionally threatening, Cassandra-like, then once more summoning us with a moralistic and pedagogical undertone. Political demands thrust their way into the domain of individual morality and individual lifestyle. This is a symptom of vast importance. It shows in fact that the classical bourgeois distinction between public and private is in a new way open to discussion. Not, of course, open to dissolution (this would only be possible at the cost of the political negation of the individual), but certainly open to be shaped in a new way. This new configuration must obviously take place at the grassroots of society. This is, in fact, the place where political life with its new demands becomes a personal reality, and a personal feeling of involvement can itself become a political reality. It is the place where politics and morality can be reconciled again in a nontotalitarian fashion. This would thereby become the starting point for the anthropological revolution.

Of course, in the meantime a growing number of groups have emerged at the grassroots level of society, groups seeking or already practicing alternative lifestyles in response to the challenge posed by the question of survival. Among these are certainly quite a few escapists fleeing into an apolitical way of life, seeking a naive counterculture based on political innocence. But there are many others who are really combining their struggle for a new way of life, a new lifestyle, with political responsibility; they are working, so to speak, in everyday political life for a new configuration of the relationship between public and private concerns. Among these are yet other groups who "live differently" in terms of an explicitly Christian motivation. It would be important in my view to see in these various groups and initiatives not only the usual outsiders (who appear continually in every society and in every church), but also the heralds of a new political culture being experienced in a still highly diffuse form. If they remain alone, they will soon lose whatever narrow political potential they now possess, they will disintegrate and be absorbed again by that total societal context of life which is the very thing needing to be transformed. Left by themselves, they are obviously incapable of being the bearers of the revolution we have been discussing.

But what would happen if our main churches themselves would at last take on more diversified forms at the grassroots level? If they were to form of themselves something like basic communities, or at least allow these more and more to exist, no longer viewing them simply as a product of the churches of the Third World, as being nontransferable to us and specific to the third-world state of development? Such a development is blocked among us above all by the ideal of the "purely religious parish community." Yet the latter is, in far too massive a way, the organizational reflex of the church as bourgeois religion. It mirrors, in far too great a degree, the bourgeois distinction between public and private for it to be capable of contributing substantially to a transformation of this distinction. In addition, reasons of pastoral necessity have long since rationalized the ideal of the purely religious parish community. We hear time and again that the introduction of conflicts at the grassroots level would only disturb the peace of the parish communities. As if community in the Lord's Supper made invisible the sufferings of society and the challenges this involves for those sharing in the eucharistic meal, when, in fact, it renders these realities uniquely visible.

In the meantime, the high price we are paying in our parish communities for this kind of social indifference and pretended political neutrality becomes ever more clear. All too often, by the avoidance of social differences and the ironing out of grassroots diversity, these communities show the very features they were meant to overcome: such as the alienation and lack of contact among the churchgoers themselves, about which we hear ever-increasing complaints. Perhaps there lies waiting in this increasingly obvious crisis of our churches an opportunity for radical change in their understanding of parish community. Just as in the Latin American church, the basic communities combine together prayer and political struggle, the Eucharist and work for liberation, so in our context basic communities could and should develop as the motive force and the manifestation of that anthropological revolution which is nourished by the power of the Eucharist.

Of course, even a base-community church could itself never become the sole bearer of such an anthropological revolution. Christians would have to follow a path here with many others, with many unbelievers also, who seek this revolution from motives which are totally different from those of Christians. And they would all have to reckon with many setbacks and many defeats.

Yet will we, in fact, have enough time to embark on this anthropological revolution? Enough time for the interplay between new praxis and a revolutionary change of consciousness? Enough time to find a way forward — one which avoids disaster — in humanity's present crisis of survival? Have we not already been standing for ages with the water almost over our heads? This indeed seems to be the case. And that is why I am far from certain that we will have sufficient time. However, my final commentary on this will be a reference to Martin Luther — to the famous answer he gave when he was asked what he would do if he knew that tomorrow the world would end. He replied: "I would plant a tree in my garden." In my opinion, that answer is neither the expression of a feeble resignation to fate, nor an attitude of apocalyptic gloating. It is rather the expression of the cold-bloodedness proper to Christian hope. Without the latter we will certainly not risk that anthropological revolution, for which we as Christians are strengthened by the bread of life.

Chapter 5

Theology Today

New Crises and New Visions

I would like to deal with two topics. The first of these offers some reflections on theology and the Church, that is, theology as it grapples with the future of the Church. The second concerns theology and society, that is, theology as it is challenged by the so-called project of modernity.

I

For many, the last Council seemed to belong to the past even before it was concluded. I myself was once of this opinion. I was mistaken. The question, How to be faithful to the inheritance of the Second Vatican Council, is a life-and-death question for the Church. This becomes clear when we look at the Church as a whole, and when we are on our guard against ethnocentric fallacies. If I am not mistaken, then there are two different, even seemingly opposed visions of the future of the Church which are currently engaged in a struggle with one another. These competing visions are becoming ever more focused upon the question of how to be faithful to the last Council. Will a backward glancing vision which longs for a pre-Reformation Western Christianity attain dominance? Or will a vision dominate which tries to save the irreplaceable tradition of the Western Church in conjunction with the innovations within the emerging churches? Will a defensive or an offensive strategy for saving traditions prevail? A traditionalist or a nontraditionalist handing on of the Council?

Presently, Rome seems to be putting all signals on hold, "playing it safe." Does playing it safe, however, mean to favor a course of immunization, that is, pastoral finger-in-the-dike strategies? Or can there not be something like an offensive tutiorism, by which I mean the saving of Christian identity through courageous self-reform of the Church? Not only the Church but society as well desires to play it safe. We are skeptical of great visions and we are reluctant to initiate major changes. Could not the Church in such a situation demonstrate her authentic noncontemporary nature by realizing her reformational potential? Is not timely self-reformation a grace, when opposed to the danger of being changed by the anonymous pressure of contemporary consensus?

It would be superficial to describe these two competing visions with the antagonism between conservative and progressive points of view. Such a comparison gives the false impression that the offensive strategy would succumb to a traditionless *aggiornamento* or to a traitorous subjection to the *Zeitgeist*. The paradigm for an offensive handing on of the Council is not undialectical modernization or liberalization but radicalization, that is, the attempt of the Church to lay hold of its roots.

In this sense the last Council can be viewed as "the beginning of a beginning" (Karl Rahner) which challenges today's theology. Some years ago I maintained that faithfulness to the Council demands a "second courage" on the part of theologians. I have two theses to clarify this offensive paradigm.

First Thesis

The last Council aims at the transition from a culturally monocentric Western Church to a culturally polycentric world Church. This binds contemporary theology to be on guard against ethnocentric fallacies and to develop the consequences of this transition.

What is the import of the experience that the Church no longer simply "has" a Third World Church but "is" a Third World Church with its origins and its constitutive history in the West (and in Europe)? In order to at least hint at the theological importance of this development I would like to divide hypothetically the previous ecclesial and theological history into three epochs: At first, a relatively short foundational epoch of Judeo-Christianity; second, a very long epoch within a more or less homogeneous culture, namely the period of Christianity which developed out of the Hellenistic context and the Western and European culture and civilization which up to our time is connected with it; and finally, the epoch of a worldwide cultural polycentrism in Church and theology which is currently manifesting itself. The Church has arrived at a transition from an Occidental European Church, which actually could only simulate a world Church, to a worldwide Church with a culturally polycentric character. Only in this worldwide Church is there a historical clarification as to what is intended with this apostolic mission with which we are confronted in the first church history — in the Acts of the Apostles: You shall be my witnesses even to the ends of the earth (Acts 1).

The Second Vatican Council opened the way for this transition to a polycentric world Church. Let me briefly mention some elements of the Council which point to this conclusion:

- The first Council with native bishops from the nonwestern world
- The major local churches once again attain their autonomy within the universal Church
- The use of the vernacular languages in the reformed liturgy
- Impulses in the doctrinal statements of the Council:

  The Decree on Religious Freedom with its principle of tolerance: the Church proclaims itself as a religious institution of freedom which in its proclamation of the gospel renounces all prior power which would negate this freedom.

  The Decree concerning the Relationship to the Non-Christian Religions in which for the first time non-Christian religions were positively evaluated and were not merely apologetically delimited.

  The statements in the *Pastoral Constitution on the Church*, in which, perhaps still defused and rather implicit, an understanding of the world is at work which begins to break with the over-identification of the world with the Occidental European world.

When we take these elements into account, we see that theology and the Church are facing the end of their more or less cultural monocentrism. Of course, this end does not mean the dissolution into an arbitrary, contextual pluralism, nor the enthronement of a new non-European monocentrism in the Church and in theology. The historical development of the West remains inherent to the new cultural polycentrism of the Church and of theology. Nevertheless, we are concerned here with reciprocal inspiration in developing the life of Church and theology. Theology can no longer divide the situation of Church and theology in two parts. This has, in my opinion, several consequences.

I would like briefly to clarify this polycentrism with respect to the situation in Latin America. Even though one may suggest that Latin America is not the best example of cultural polycentrism within the Church because it is too close to European culture, we should not forget that mutual inspiration and creative assimilation between the various cultures is possible only if they are not completely alien and distant from each other. If we analyze the present struggle within the Latin American churches we find that in principle they do not represent a contrast between an orthodox position eagerly and uncompromisingly defending the traditions of the Church on the one hand, and on the other a liberation church more or less suspected of false teachings and of being influenced by strange political ideology. Rather these wranglings reflect the painful transition from a Eurocentric to a culturally polycentric Church of the world.

I would like to outline the consequences of this new polycentric situation for Western theology. First of all, the social antagonism in the world is pulled into the center of ecclesial and theological interest. Conditions which are in direct opposition to the gospel, such as exploitation, oppression, racism, become a challenge for theology; they demand the formulation of faith in categories of nonviolent resistance and change. Thus theology becomes political out of its own *logos*. Second, European theology has to understand itself within the horizon of a history of guilt. While Western theology should not indulge in neurotic self-accusations, this history of guilt should not be forgotten either. Frequently, we protect ourselves against it by all types of defense mechanisms: for example, with the help of a "tactical provincialism" with which we try to safeguard our church and political life against global influence; or when we talk of the countries of the Third World as our underdeveloped partners, but hardly ever as our victims. The theological sensitivity to the new culturally polycentric world Church will teach us to judge ourselves and our own history with the eyes of our victims. Thus theology in the new paradigm must become a politically sensitive theology of penance and conversion. I have critically described a Western Christianity which closes its mind to this experience as "bourgeois religion."

Finally, our Western theology faces the challenge of a new awakening in and from the poor churches of the world. Theology has to make public this charismatic shock within the universal Church. As I see it, there is a threefold reformational thrust:

1. The development of a new ecclesial model in the so-called basic communities which are in connection with the bishops and thus are included in the apostolic succession.

2. The concentration on discipleship, resulting in a politically sensitive spirituality with a preferential option for the poor. In specific distinction to other world religions, as a Christian one can be too pious and too mystical! The one and undivided discipleship of Jesus always contains a mystical and a situational political element. They mirror one another, and that is specifically Christian!

3. The theological impulse concerning a new vital unity of redemption and liberation in which the experience of resistance and suffering returns to the experience of grace. In facing this challenge Western Catholic theology must not forget one thing: There is something like a European dilemma of Catholicism. The Catholic Church accompanied the European history of modern times more or less defensively. It did not really productively participate in the so-called history of modern freedom, especially not in the development of civic Enlightenment. Most of the time

it exclusively opposed these processes. The overcoming of this Catholic dilemma in the late European situation, at least for me, points beyond the Occidental-European monocultural church life toward a world Church which learns how to call for and to represent the grace of God as an undivided liberation of humankind and which willingly pays the price for this historic conjugation of grace and freedom.

One of the central questions for Church and theology today is: Will we understand the socially divided and polycentric world as that learning space in which we find many signs of a Christianity, which, in the face of great danger, lays hold of its roots? This question guides my interest in the handing on of the impulses of Vatican II.

Before I present my second thesis, I would like to touch on some questions which arise in the context of this first thesis.

First: The transition to a polycentric world Church makes possible and also demands a clarification of the constitutive truth of Western Christianity. We are here not paying tribute to a stylish anti-European attitude, nor to a cheap criticism of so-called Eurocentrism. Especially in the face of this cultural polycentrism, we can recognize that the Western inheritance has its roots in two cultures, in two traditions. It is not only the Greek Hellenistic inspiration, structured and developed in the Roman legal framework, but also the inheritance of Palestine, the Jewish tradition, which gave birth to Western Christianity. It is not only the God of Athens but primarily the God of Jerusalem who has to put his stamp on that Western Christianity which remains constitutive for a culturally polycentric world Church. Did not the recent instruction of the Holy Office concerning some questions of liberation theology one-sidedly overemphasize the Hellenistic tradition with its historic dualism? Has not the God of Moses been forgotten in favor of the God of Plato? I will return to the actuality of the Jewish elements in Western Christianity in the last part of my address.

Second: The polycentrism thesis implies a number of specific problems. For instance, I presuppose that there actually still is this kind of cultural polycentricity in the world. In other words, I have to assume that this polycentricity is not already affected in its roots by that profane westernization of the entire world, which we call technological development or technological civilization — in short by the world conquest accomplished by Western rationality. Is there still enough cultural identity and resistance to the global process of Western secularization? Is not every liberation of these non-Western countries in the last analysis merely a liberation into the arms of Western civilization? Especially with respect to the African and Asian cultures there arise problems for theology insofar as these cultures are already expressions of great world religions.

The polycentrism thesis, therefore, also demands a new paradigm for the dialogue with non-Christian religions.

Third: How can Christian universalism be understood so that it does not imperialistically absorb these religions and cultures, but rather acknowledges them in their own dignity, as the Second Vatican Council teaches? In my critique of Karl Rahner's abstract universality in his theory of "anonymous Christianity" I propose a narrative-practical expression of this Christian universality which avoids the dangers of intellectual imperialism. The abstract universalism in the theory of anonymous Christianity can be unmasked in view of the Jews: the Jews can never be viewed as anonymous Christians because, according to Paul, Israel as such belongs to Christian eschatology.

Second Thesis

The Second Vatican Council aims at a transition from a Church of dependents to a Church of agents or subjects, (that is from a *Kirche für das Volk* to a *Kirche des Volkes* or from a *Betreuungskirche* to a *Subjektkirche, eine Kirche mit einer subjekthaften Basis*) and this transition demands from theology that it not only respect the teaching office of the Church but also the teaching authority of the faithful.

The formulation of the thesis itself calls for a brief semantic clarification. I have not found an adequate English term to translate the German word *Subjekt*. *Subjekt* is not equivalent to "person" or "individual." Rather, *Subjekt* connotes the person insofar as it is individualized by means of social and historical intersubjectivity. This implies a constitutional and chronic vulnerability of the individual. In this sense, the word "subject" does not refer to the isolated individual, the monad who only afterwards made sure of his existence with other subjects. Experiences of solidarity with, antagonism toward, liberation from, and anxiety about other subjects form an essential part of the constitution of the religious subject, not afterwards, but from the very beginning.

Normally the principle of collegiality is considered to be the most wide-reaching thrust of the Council with regard to inner-ecclesial renewal. Although I recognize the importance and the practical relevance of this principle, my thesis suggests a different starting point. I begin with the fact that *Lumen gentium* tends toward a definitely subject-oriented understanding of Church. The dominant images are neither of the Pauline and patristic type, such as *corpus Christi* (the mystical body) the wine and the branches or the ark, nor of the modern type such as *Ursakrament* or *sacramentum mundi*, though the latter play a definite part in the document. Instead the biblically rooted image of the people of God on their pilgrimage through history is central. Such an image is centered upon the people faced with historical experiences of suffering and struggle and thus it points toward what I call a subject-oriented vision of the Church, that is, a vision in which *all* the faithful insofar as they are Church are called to become subjects. Together with this understanding of the Church the Council emphasizes the active role of the faithful in articulating and developing the authentic witness to the gospel. The Council treats the faithful not as merely passive recipients of ecclesial teaching but rather as active subjects in the Church insofar as the teaching of the Church is based on the witness of the whole of the people of God (cf. *Lumen gentium* 12, 37; *Dei verbum* 10; *Apostolicam actuositatem* 2, 3; *Gaudium et spes* 43).

I would like to point to another line of argumentation of the Council which converges with this subject-oriented thrust. In *The Decree on Religious Freedom* the Council proclaims the transition from the dignity of truth to the dignity of person in truth. The abstract subordination of the person to a truth without a subject is abandoned for a subject-oriented basis of truth. The struggle for the dignity of the subject in the Church is not understood as being freed from the truth but as being freed for the truth of the gospel (*Nicht Befreiung von der Wahrheit, sondern Befreiung zur Wahrheit des Glaubens*). This statement also points toward a subject-oriented understanding of the Church.

The Council does not speak expressly of a teaching authority and a teaching competence of the faithful. It speaks expressly only of the teaching office that is imbedded in the entire organism of the people of God. I also do not speak of the magisterium of the faithful but of their teaching authority which remains in the background within the usual division of labor in the Church. This usual division of labor may be expressed — perhaps all too briefly — thus: the bishops teach — the priests serve — theologians clarify and defend the teaching and train those who serve. And the people? They are for the most part the "object" of this teaching and serving Church. The image of the Church implied in this division of labor is that of the Church of dependents (*Betreuungskirche*). Theology working in terms of this division of labor reproduces *nolens volens* this system of dependency or a system of services. The image of the Church of dependents is not simply canonical and it is already overcome in the ecclesial vision of Vatican II. The statements of the Council point to an understanding of the Church in which the Church as a whole is a learning and a teaching Church. In virtue of their lived faith (*sensus fidelium*) an authentic authority is attributed to the faithful. They are considered as active subjects of their faith and of its theologically relevant expression.

That we are dealing here with an authentic renewal can be demonstrated through a brief historical reflection. Already in the New Testament one can see a tension regarding the determination of the decision-makers in the Church: The Pastoral Epistles, on the one hand, emphasize the competence of individual church officials, whereas the rest of the New Testament favors the entire community as the bearer of the decision-making responsibility in the Church. After the first several centuries the teaching authority of the community is gradually absorbed by the teaching office of the bishops. In the Middle Ages there is a teaching authority alongside of the teaching office of the bishops. But this teaching authority is heavily intellectualized; it is the teaching authority of the experts, that is the *Doctores*. This intellectual teaching authority, based on the knowledge of experts, was strengthened in the processes of modernity, especially in the Enlightenment, and thus consolidated an understanding of the teaching authority which is based on an opposition between experts and people. The vision of the Second Vatican Council transcends this model of the dependency of the faithful. This has consequences for theology, for ecumenism, and for the present societal struggle for the dignity of the subject.

A. As far as theology is concerned I see primarily two consequences. The first of these deals with an appropriate understanding of orthodoxy. For theology which reproduces, however sublimely, a Church of dependents, the orthodoxy of the people can only be explained by a theory of *bona fides* or in particular by a theory *offices implicita*. Full and explicit knowledge of faith is, after all, *a practical knowledge!* In its distinctive character, it is incommensurable with an elitist idealistic gnosiology. It is possible to speak of an arcane knowledge in the case of a full knowledge of faith, but this *arcanum* cannot be the *arcanum* of a philosophical gnosis but must be the *arcanum* of a practical knowledge. It cannot be the *arcanum* of a Socrates, but must be the *arcanum* of Jesus, in other words, the practical arcane knowledge of following Christ.

Christian orthodoxy is in its essence not an elite form of orthodoxy in which the little ones can only participate *bona fides* or *fides implicita* (Luke 10:21 and Matt. 11:25). The contents of faith and their teaching are themselves practical. The idea of God to which Christian orthodoxy binds us is itself a practical idea. The stories of exodus, of conversion, of resistance and suffering belong to its *doctrinal* expression. The pure idea of God is, in reality, an abbreviation, a shorthand for stories without which there is no Christian truth in this idea of God. This also applies to christological orthodoxy. At its core is once again practical knowledge. At its center is not an idea to which one must assent, but a story, not an entertaining story but rather a dangerous one, a story not only to be told but to be lived. Its saving truth is revealed only in this living practice.

The infallibility of the whole Church which Vatican II emphasizes means that the Church will never betray this practical knowledge.

From this follow two consequences. (1) Christian orthodoxy is not simply an arcane knowledge of the magisterium or a knowledge of experts which molds the faithful into passive recipients and thus prevents them from being living subjects of the faith. In addition, it becomes clear that the teaching authority of the faithful must be recognized and developed because they belong to the guarantors of this type of orthodoxy. The modes of expression of the faithful must be cultivated. Theirs is neither the doctrinal language of the shepherds nor the argumentative language of the experts, but rather the narrative language, the oral history, or other modes of expression which are not simply deficient modes of expressing orthodoxy.

There are examples in the present situation of the Church for the recognition of the practical teaching authority of the faithful. Here I am not only thinking of the Latin American basic communities in which the people in connection with their bishops and theologians attempt to formulate creedal statements which reflect their practical faith. If I am not mistaken, the recent attempts of the American bishops to develop their pastoral letters through an exchange with the believing communities point in the same direction. For me, it is symptomatic that Rome, as far as I have heard, had problems not so much with the contents of these letters on peace and the economy, but with the procedures by which these letters came to be.

(2) Naturally, I know that this "consulting the faithful in matters of doctrine" implies great problems that Newman did not pursue further, as he maintained in his famous *Rambler* article that during the Arian controversy not the bishops, but the faithful in spite of the bishops saved orthodoxy. What do we understand today under Newman's term "the mass of the faithful"? How do we determine today the convictions of the faithful? Demoscopically? A public opinion poll in *Time* magazine? Would we then learn more than mere suburban middle-class values and expectations? More than, let me say, the diffuse and vague opinions and options brought about by the turbulent pluralism of our hearts and minds? On the one hand, this pluralistic situation allows us to recognize the meaning and necessity of a magisterium: In an ever-more mobile and historical world a truth which is based on memory and tradition cannot be saved without institutionalization. On the other hand, there is a twofold danger. First, all truths of faith are accessible only in a magisterially and ecclesiologically encoded fashion. For example: already Vatican II, as opposed to Vatican I, teaches the central truths of the faith not in themselves, but as elements of ecclesiology. The danger

of an ecclesiological narcissism emerges which forgets that the center of the Church is never the Church herself. Second, in the face of this pluralistic situation, the Church of dependents stabilizes itself once again and thus succumbs to the temptation to explain everything in terms of the *fides implicita*, which according to Newman induces indifference in the intellectuals and superstition in the masses.

What are we to do? For me, this is one of the key problems of the Church and of theology today. I know of only one way: We can go beyond the Church of dependents only when the dependents transform themselves. We cannot beg for authority of the faithful from the hierarchy. Have the faithful not interiorized the paternalistic Church to such an extent that they think everything connected with church renewal ultimately depends on one thing: on change happening to those who take care of them, which means, above all, the pope and the bishops? The fact is, a dependent people has to transform itself, and not just behave like a people being taken care of. Is not much of the usual criticism of the Church just another expression of the interiorized paternalistic Church? Is it not fixated to an inordinate extent on authority, and, if possible, on papal authority? On the contrary! If things are to get better in the Church, it will depend before everything else on the faithful themselves. The faithful should believe themselves capable of a greater measure of the gospel and require it of themselves. They should therefore overcome, at least within themselves, that lack of repentance and self-criticism which they deplore in the Church, especially in regard to the church hierarchy.

Therefore, it is of special importance for theology to watch for symptoms of this transformation and to stabilize them. It is important to reflect theologically upon the emergence of a new model of ecclesial life which is appearing today alongside the traditional types of the paternalistic and services Church, namely the basic community church with its new culture of communication and solidarity. This basic community church is neither a passing fad, nor an adaptation from the Third World; it is instead a legitimate ecclesial expression of the conciliar truth which calls for a subject church with a legitimate teaching authority of the faithful. Naturally this new type of ecclesial identity has many pastoral and theological implications and raises a series of questions regarding currently prevailing church ordinances which I cannot consider here.

Instead, I must turn to a further consequence for theology which flows from my second thesis. The transition to a subject church and to the recognition of a teaching authority of the faithful aims at a widening and a differentiation of the agents of theology and a new paradigm of theological activity. This new theological activity corresponds to the emerging type of ecclesial identity. In comparison to our academic theology this type is marked by a certain theological poverty, sometimes even by a refusal of the prevailing theology. This ought not to be grounds for us simply to ignore this new type of theology. The literary genre of this theology is not the theological textbook but a kind of report or logbook, the literary manifesto of new paths with the Church and in the Church. Naturally this kind of theology does not wish to replace academic theology but to supplement it in that this new theology, for example, forces upon the collective memory of the Church, the often unspoken yet concrete experiences of discipleship, the sorrow and the struggle of the people.

Allow me to name some important elements of this type of theological activity. First, this type demonstrates that the primary subjects of critique in the Church are not the theologians but the believers. In this sense, I understand, for example, the grassroots theology in the poor countries as an attempt to make public the cry of the poor so that it reaches the ear of the whole Church and its magisterium. When the Latin American bishops in Puebla interpret their teaching as the voice of the voiceless, then they recognize something like a teaching authority of the poor and of the voiceless in the Church. In order that this representation of the poor by the bishops does not become a religious instrumentalization of the poor and of their suffering-derived wisdom, this theology has to see to it that these poor themselves increasingly become subjects of their life, their history, and their very fragile world of religious symbols.

Second, this new theological activity helps to formulate and develop short formulas of faith. Such short formulas cannot, in my opinion, be dictated by theological master thinkers. Christian faith cannot be compressed into a doctrinal formula without a subject. Its center lies rather between doctrine and praxis: in what we call, with an abbreviation, discipleship. Therefore, there are short formulas of faith only when teaching and life, doxography, and biography are pressed into one. This new theological paradigm can already provide examples of this. I have already mentioned the attempts of the basic communities to spell out their faith experience in creedal statements.

Finally, this theological activity could offer the whole Church and her magisterium new accents in the proclamation of church teaching. For example, the Church could learn perhaps that her proclamation to today's world must not center primarily upon the justification of the sinful people in the face of the almighty and good God (represented by the Church), but must center upon the justification of God in the face of a creation torn and disfigured by suffering and injustice which cries out to heaven, that is, must center upon the theodicy question.

My support for this new theological activity cannot be a matter of romantic idealization or archaic reductionism. The classic form of theology serves, for example, to integrate the new experiences in the Church and the new praxis into the total memory of the Church; it thus prevents these experiences from remaining merely sporadic and ultimately disintegrating. It confronts these new experiences with all the reserves of experience and faith which are laid up in the Church; it thus mediates to the grass roots that support of tradition without which there is no truly Christian experience and no consistent resistance. It also takes care — as academic theology — that the "base of the church" does not descend to the cognitive isolation of a sect.

Nevertheless, I would like to clarify one point which makes the teaching authority of the faithful especially important for us as academic theologians. Our theological argumentation today is more and more confronted with scientific theories which are no longer innocent over and against theology and the Church. These theories see themselves, though with variant degrees of explicitness, as so-called metatheories of religion and theology. For them, theology can be analyzed and subsumed within a more general theoretical system. It is the system of evolutionary logic which considers religion as an important stage within the evolution of humankind, albeit one which has already been surpassed.

Theology's response to such theories cannot be to seek a foundation and justification in a further attempt to produce a more general "pure" theory from its own resources. In order to avoid the risk of a speculative infinite regression, which would inevitably have to be broken off arbitrarily at some point, it must look for its basis in terms of a return to the subjects of faith and their practice. This return would only then be regressive and undifferentiated if there were no authentic intelligibility of the praxis of the faithful, an intelligibility which cannot be replaced by theological reflection. In order to set this intelligibility free academic theology must transcend the system of the Church of dependents in which the faithful must remain silent or merely reproduce a predetermined theology.

B. This second thesis has further relevance in two areas: first of all, an ecumenical relevance. It is obvious that the recognition of the subject church and of the teaching authority of the faithful in the Church is an important step toward the self-reform of the Church. And this self-reform is itself a necessary step in the growth of Christian unity (if one does not consider the ecumenical question just a question of gnosiology, but as a question of practical change of the churches).

The second area of relevance: In the development of this inheritance of the Council theology enters into the struggle against the so-called death of the subject in the project of modernity. There is, on the one hand, the danger of a placid death of the subject. Modern scientific knowledge is *per definitionem* not founded upon a subject-oriented basis of knowledge. The human being as a subject is treated as an anthropomorphism. Thus the talk about the death of God is followed today by the talk about the death of the subject in so-called postmodernity. There are also symptoms, on the other hand, for a dramatic death of the subject. Wherever, as in the Marxist countries, the difference between state and society, public and private is denied in principle, the subject as an individual can then only be understood as a potential saboteur of this order. But also in the West there is already a discussion concerning the successor to the human being as subject. As you know, *Time* magazine has already portrayed this successor on its cover: the robot, a smoothly functioning machine, a computerized intelligence which cannot remember because it cannot forget, that is, an intelligence without memories, without pathos and morals, in short without an identity as a subject.

II

My concluding reflection focuses on theology in the face of the so-called project of modernity, insofar as the undialectical continuation of this project results not only in the death of the subject but also in the death of history, both of which are an encoded form of the death of God. Over and against this tendency within late modernity theology has to mobilize that dangerous memory which has its source primarily in the proscribed or misunderstood apocalyptic tradition. That is, in a word, my proposal. One of the key elements of my theological enterprise is the attempt to recapture the sense of the unsettling apocalyptic question whose proscription is the presupposition of the project of modernity. In concluding, I would like, therefore, to hand this question over to you. I know that it contains a challenge to the theological adventure of being noncontemporary. In order that this experience of being noncontemporary does not degenerate into mere blind or aggressive backwardness, but rather remains creative, we dare not leave it to the fundamentalists and traditionalists.

The fact that even theologians and preachers use the apocalyptic symbols today as free-floating metaphors and project them onto the present fears of nuclear world catastrophe does not demonstrate their present relevance, but shows, in my opinion, how repressed and misunderstood they are. Not because the apocalyptic question is considered relevant today, but because its seeming actuality confirms how forgotten it is, the apocalyptic question must be posed anew. Allow me to attempt this.

"Who is close to me is close to the fire, who is far from me is far from the Kingdom." I understand this noncanonical word, transmitted to us by Origen, as an abbreviated commentary on the apocalyptic of the New Testament. It is dangerous to be close to Jesus, yet only in the face of danger shines the vision from the Kingdom of God, which through him has come closer. "Danger" apparently is a basic category in which to experience his life and his message and to define Christian identity. The lightning of danger illuminates the entire biblical landscape, especially the New Testament. Danger and peril are found everywhere in the New Testament. In John we read: "Remember the word I said unto you: The servant is not greater than his Lord. If they have persecuted me they will persecute you" (John 15:8–9). And in Paul: "We are troubled on every side, but not distressed; we are perplexed but not in despair, persecuted but not forsaken; cast down but not destroyed" (2 Cor. 4:8–9). How can we understand the New Testament, if in our interpretations the presence of danger is systematically disregarded, in other words, if we do not apply a hermeneutic of danger, if we erase the horizon of danger or paint it over — that horizon which holds together the whole New Testament panorama?

What is behind our modern critique of the apocalyptic symbols of danger and crisis? Is it the will toward enlightenment of the uncomprehended power of myth in this tradition, or is it perhaps the will to evade the dangerous Christ and so to contain the danger, or at least to push it aside into the practically extraterritorial realm of individual death? Most likely both of these are at work. Above all we cannot forget this evasion and there are many attempts to interpret the whole of history after Christ as a maneuver to evade the dangerous Christ. In the context of this evasion arises a Christianity — and I say this not in a denouncing manner but rather with a touch of sadness and helplessness — there arises a Christianity fashioned after a bourgeois homeland religion, rid of danger but also rid of consolation. For a Christianity which is not dangerous and unendangered also does not console. Or am I grossly mistaken? In some regions of today's Christianity I see emerging counterimages to such a placatingly "bürgerliche Religion." For example, in those poor churches which understand their faithfulness to Christ also as liberation, and as liberation seek it in the face of the greatest danger. This church is connected with early Christianity by the red thread of martyrdom and by the power of a temporal expectation in God's faithfulness. Who could possibly doubt that here a clearer concept breaks forth of what it means to be close to Jesus, to be close to him of whom it should be said: "Who is close to me is close to the fire"?

The fatal disease of religion and theology is not naiveté, but rather banality. Theology can become banal whenever its commentary on life serves only to repeat that which without it — and often against it —

has already become part of modern common consent (modern common-place). The naiveté of theology lies in ambush for these commonplaces. It does this, for example, by lingering with texts and images such as those in the apocalyptic traditions and by holding its own in the face of them at least a bit longer than modern consent and the anonymous pressure of modern civilization allows. Theology does not seek specifically to reconcile itself with its traditions by the use of thousands of subtle modifications, but rather to spell out its tradition as dangerous, subversive memory for the present.

Religion, in pointing to the apocalyptic symbols, wants to scandalize (interrupt, provoke) the dominant understanding of the human being in modernity, and to resist this understanding at least for one brief moment. It seeks to interrupt that image of the human being which is prevalent today within all blocks: the Faustian-Promethean human being. It seeks to interrupt that concept in which the coming human being is designed without the dark background of sorrow, suffering, guilt, and death. The rebellion of the apocalyptic symbols is turned against the human being empty of secrets, incapable of mourning and therefore incapable of being consoled; more and more unable to remember and so more easily manipulated than ever; more and more defenseless against the threatening apotheosis of banality and against the stretched out death of boredom; a human being whose dreams of happiness finally are nothing but the dreams of an unhappiness free from suffering and longing.

Religion, in pointing to the apocalyptic symbols, wants to interrupt (scandalize) the dominant understanding of time and history in modernity and to resist it at least for one brief moment. This resistance, this kind of interruption of our common consent, is even more difficult to understand and practically not able to be freed from the suspicion of being deviant. No wonder that most theologians agree with the modern consent and that they see in these apocalyptic texts and symbols nothing but the projection of archaic fears.

Whenever religion hands down (passes on) these texts and symbols and perceives in them elements of a dangerous memory, it does not do it in order to comment on the course of world history with an apocalyptically infused gloating, but in order to discover the sources of our modern fear.

It may be that the archaic human being was always endangered by the feeling of an imminent end of his life and world (and we can see something of this also in the present fear of catastrophes). But, in my opinion, for modern man there is not primarily a fear that everything will come to an end, but a more deeply rooted fear that there will be no end at all, that our life and our history is pulled into the surging of a faceless evolution which finally rolls over us all, as over grains of sand on the beach.

There is a cult today of the makeable — everything can be made. There is also a new cult of fate — everything can be replaced. The will to make is undermined by resignation. The cult of the omnipotent control of man's destiny on the one hand, and the cult of apathy on the other belong together like two sides of the same coin. Man's understanding of reality, which guides his scientific and technical control of nature and from which the cult of the makeable draws its strength, is marked by an idea of time as a continuous process which is empty and evolving toward infinity and within which everything is enclosed without grace. This understanding of reality excludes all expectation and therefore produces that fatalism that eats away our soul. We, therefore, are already resigned to this even before society has been able to introduce us successfully to this resignation as a form of pragmatic rationality. This understanding of time generates that secret fear of identity which can be deciphered only with great difficulty because it is successfully practiced under the ciphers of progress and development, before we may, just for a fleeting moment, discover it at the base of our souls.

This timeless time is the secret Lord of late modernity. The great utopias become stranded on this timeless time. In the East as well as in the West today, politics are characterized by a lack of great visions. Short-term strategies prevail over long-term ones. The secret fear of timeless time is the cause for that phenomenon which has been called the cynicism of late modernity: the cult of apathy in which people exercise the art of alibi: They do not want to take on dangerous responsibilities, they play possum, they stick their heads in the sand in the face of danger or they become voyeurs (spectators) of their own downfall. For me, these are symptoms of an evolutionary poisoned lassitude about history. How could Christianity subject itself to the anonymous pressure of the posthistoric in late modernity and thus move from the field of history to that of psychology without losing its own identity?

Has not a type of bland Christian eschatology, that is, an eschatology without apocalyptic sting, prepared the way for this timeless time? Has not this eschatology, in the name of the triumph of Christ, cleansed time of all its contradictions and ironed out all catastrophes? Has it not interpreted all dangerous and catastrophic downfalls as the soft echo of a departing thunderstorm? Has it not contributed to an understanding of time as an empty and surprise-free endless continuum, as a timeless time in which the second coming of Christ cannot even be conceived? However, because we as Christians believe in a saving end of time, we can and must dare to have an authentic historic consciousness, that is, the confrontation with the abyss, with radical discontinuity. We can and must risk a memory which remembers not only what has succeeded but also what has been destroyed, not only what has been achieved, but also what has been lost and in this way is turned against the identification of the semantic potential of history with the victory of what has become and already exists. This is a dangerous memory. It saves the Christian continuum. And it demonstrates that the *memoria passionis* in its anamnetic solidarity with the defeated, with the past sufferings, becomes a universal category, a category of rescue: saving the dignity of history and of the human subjects acting and suffering in history.

The biblical God has always allied himself with those who, according to an endless evolution and its pressure of selection, should have no history, no future. This is true from the alliance of God with the weak, insignificant tribes of Israel to the alliance of God with the defeated Jesus of Nazareth on the cross. I do not see how we can hinder the absorption of history, which is always God's history with us, into a timeless time without reclaiming the apocalyptic dimension of our Christian eschatology. That is why I hand on to you the question of an as yet undisclosed, suppressed truth in the apocalyptic symbols.

Part 2

Theology as Interruption

Chapter 6

Between Evolution and Dialectics

The Point of Departure
for a Contemporary Fundamental Theology

"Always be prepared to make a defense to anyone who calls you to account for the hope that is in you" (1 Pet. 3:15). Any Christian theology, then, can be defined, at least in its task and intention, as a defense of hope.[1] What is the hope that is in question here? It is the solidarity of hope in the God of the living and the dead, who calls all men to be his subjects. In our defense of this hope, we are concerned not with a conflict between ideas unrelated to any subject, but rather with the concrete historical and social situation in which subjects are placed, with their experiences, sufferings, struggles, and contradictions.

The Need to Analyze the Situation
and the Special Features of This Analysis

If we are concerned, then, with the human situation,[2] we have first to analyze this situation, since we cannot expect an analysis to be provided in advance either by theology or by any standardized philosophy. The various concrete aspects of this analysis of the situation are then examined separately in the discussion of different themes in the second part of the book. This is done in order to avoid an artificial separation between characterizing the situation and reflecting upon it theologically.

---

1. One of the most important aspects of the task of the explicit Christian today is to make a defense of hope. This is clear from the title given by the synod of German bishops to a "Confession of Faith in Our Time" (*Our Hope*) and their introductory statement in this document, describing the "defense of faith" as "the Church's task." The World Council of Churches is also preparing a document on the faith of Christians, in which the key concept is "defense of hope."

2. In this we are omitting another need that inevitably arises from our understanding of defending hope — the need to ask who is to make this defense, who is the most suitable subject of such a work of apologetics and what is the function of the professional theologian in an apologetic process which should not take place in the sphere of pure ideas and in the absence of subjects, but must be deeply involved in the experiences and sufferings of human history.

In this first section, I will confine myself to a brief, general outline of two important features of the analysis of the situation.

1. Any analysis of this situation and of the social point of departure for a Christian defense of hope must nowadays inevitably be made on a worldwide scale. Sociopolitical and economic relationships are becoming increasingly interdependent and for this reason no situation can be determined in the concrete without considering this global aspect. Any attempt to obtain a practical result without taking the global aspect into consideration will only be dubiously abstract.

It would therefore not be honest to recommend that the Latin American churches and theologians should accept an analysis of the situation that is different from the one that we would evolve for ourselves in the northern regions of the world and which would therefore produce different results. The conflict between North and South that is so extensively discussed nowadays cannot be defined or resolved in regional terms, nor can it be neutralized by the Church and theologians as a purely political and economic event. It is above all a conflict with significant effects on the one Church throughout the world.

In this context, it would be good for European theologians to take up the challenge with which they have been confronted for some time now by the Latin American theology of liberation.[3]

We can no longer simply go on exporting our Western theology to the countries of Latin America, where there are now hardly any customers who are sufficiently interested to buy it. As I see it, it is more important for Western theologians to try to see their theology within the context of worldwide processes and to take seriously the fact that it is

---

3. It is obvious that various points of contact and opportunities for a critical exchange of ideas between political theology and the theology of liberation will arise in the course of our considerations. This applies not only to their mutual insistence on an analysis of the situation on a worldwide scale, but also to many other important elements. These include a concentration on the primacy of praxis, the basic category of solidarity, and a theology of the subject based on the idea of the whole of mankind in solidarity and subjection to God. In this sense, my development of a practical political fundamental theology, in which the question not only of the situation and the point of departure, but also of the interests and the bearers of that theology is raised, is in itself an attempt to go beyond the narrow confines of central European theology or at least to define its conditioning factors and limits more clearly. L. Rütti has taken seriously the need to take this worldwide scale in political theology into account: *Zur Theologie der Mission* (Mainz and Munich, 1972). Several authors have, within the framework of political theology, been concerned with the need to interpret and communicate critically the intentions of the theology of liberation. These include the contributors (R. Almeida-Cunha, L. A. De Boni, F. Castillo, G. Süss, and others) to F. Castillo, ed., *Theologie aus der Praxis des Volkes* (Mainz and Munich, 1978), and G. Süss, *Volkskatholizismus in Brasilien* (Mainz and Munich, 1978). One article that is important in its treatment of the relationship between the theology of liberation and political theology is F. P. Fiorenza, "Political Theology and Liberation Theology: An Inquiry into their Fundamental Meaning," in *Liberation, Revolution, and Freedom: Theological Perspectives*, ed. T. M. McFadden (New York, 1975), 3–29.

conditioned by its situation within the particular context of middle-class, central European society.

2. It is also important to bear in mind that this world, which we are bound to analyze and which we tend to call the world of our experience, is in fact a secondary or meta-world, in other words, a world which, in itself and in its deepest reality, bears the deep impression of many systems and theories and which can therefore only be experienced and possibly changed in and through these systems and theories. If this fact is forgotten, the result may easily be the acceptance of an uncritical idea of praxis. A praxis which fails to take into account the complex structure of the world or our experience of it as secondary will therefore inevitably remain sporadic and ineffective. It stands symbolically for a new reality that is sought, but cannot itself bring this reality about, because it is again absorbed by the systems and theories that have become valid.

These systems, theories, or interpretations of the world, within which we experience the world itself, will be discussed more fully later on. In the meantime, however, we must content ourselves with a very brief description. On the one hand, there is the system based on an evolutionary interpretation of the world and reality, which has its roots in the Enlightenment on the one hand and our Western middle-class society on the other. On the other hand, however, there is also the historical and materialist dialectical system, which can be interpreted historically as a particular way in which the Enlightenment was realized[4] and which is manifested historically and socially above all in the socialist societies of the East.

The Apologetical and Practical Character of a Contemporary Fundamental Theology

This formal definition of a situation that is present today and has to be taken into account by theologians has important consequences. In the past, at a time when metaphysical thinking was predominant or when societies were still determined by a religious objective, it might have been possible for the theoretical points of departure that were currently valid to be simply taken over by a fundamental theology that was concerned with the theoretical foundations of Christian faith or used by that theology as a means for clarifying its own problems. This procedure is, however, no longer possible today. Neither of the two theoretical points of departure, to which all the theories that are valid today can be more or less directly traced back, is in any sense innocent or neutral with regard

---

4. See L. Goldmann, *Der christliche Bürger und die Aufklärung* (Neuwied, 1968).

to religion and Christianity and therefore also with regard to theology. They can be regarded, with different degrees of explicitness, as meta-theories with respect to religion and theology. In other words, religion can, for the purpose of these theories, in principle be either reconstructed or abolished and seen as pointing to a more comprehensive theoretical system.[5]

The Christian defense of faith, then, may come into conflict with attempts to reconstruct religion on the basis of an evolutionary theory of the world of the kind that has made a deep impression on all analytical theories of science, action, or language, to classify it adequately in accordance with quasi-evolutionary principles and in this way to give its public claim to validity a purely relative value. In this context, evolution should not be seen as a symbol leading to knowledge, but with a relevance that is confined, for example, only to the sphere of natural science. Here at least it is active as a fundamental symbol of knowledge and logic and has a theoretical status which is not clear as far as its totalizing tendency is concerned. We may, however, say quite explicitly here that evolution should certainly not be understood in this context in the sense in which it is used in everyday parlance. Nor should it be thought of as a teleologically directed development, in the sense of a nondialectical process in the advance of mankind.

We should regard evolution here rather as a basic acceptance of a technical rationality which can no longer be justified and within which structures and tendencies as well as phenomena of greater or lesser complexity are revealed and can be classified, but which is not, as a whole, capable of being further clarified and which therefore functions as a quasi-religious symbol of scientific knowledge.[6] This evolving consciousness is also active by virtue of the fact that it is already present, as a kind of feeling for life, in man's prescientific consciousness and has as such impressed itself on modern man's everyday experience of himself. Man's consciousness of his own identity has become weaker and more damaged in the course of human progress. Man is at the mercy of a darkly speckled universe and enclosed in an endless continuum of time that is no longer capable of surprising him. He feels that he is caught up in the waves of an anonymous process of evolution sweeping pitilessly over everyone. A

---

5. For a penetrating controversy with (analytical) meta-theories of theology as well as a continuation of the basic intentions of political theology, see H. Peukert, *Wissenschafts-theorie – Handlungstheorie – Fundamentale Theologie* (Düsseldorf, 1976).

6. A system orientated toward evolution, which in its wider effects can be regarded as a kind of substitute for metaphysics, may be able to classify religion, in its strictly privatized form, quite functionally into the categories of social processes. It may, for example, do this with the aim of absorbing resistance and disappointments that might endanger the course of those social processes (which are, in the last resort, without subjects).

new culture of apathy and lack of feeling is being prepared for him in view of his experience of fragile identity. It is therefore important to bear in mind the deep effects of this evolving consciousness which bears up a whole theory of the world.

Historical and dialectical materialism also claims to have seen through the strongly religious content of Christianity and to have taken over, more successfully, the liberating tendencies of the Christian religion in a secularized utopian form. This dialectical materialism must, however, become the victim of an evolutionary logic that lacks a subject, if it can only base its intention to set the world free on a teleology of freedom that is perhaps wrongly expected of matter or nature itself. I shall discuss this critical supposition later.[7] We may in any case be sure that religion and dialectics would be close to each other if they had a common opponent in the evolutionary consciousness that ultimately silences history, the subject and liberation as authentic realities. I would draw attention to two important aspects in the elaboration of a contemporary fundamental theology.

1. Any fundamental theology, which claims, as it should, to investigate the foundations of theology has an apologetical aspect, not simply incidentally or as a kind of historical survival, but as part of its essential nature. An essential task of fundamental theology, then, is to defend, justify, or give an account of the authenticity of religion, in opposition to those systems that claim to be metatheories of theology. In other words, it must do what is meant by the word "apologetics."

2. In view of these very comprehensive theories, fundamental theology of this kind cannot justify itself by developing another even more comprehensive theory which might be a theological metatheory of the existing world theories. It must, if it is to avoid a speculative regression into infinity, justify itself as theology by a return — or regression — to subjects and the praxis of subjects. In other words, it has to regard itself as a practical foundational discipline or as practical fundamental theology. As such, its task is to evoke and describe a praxis which will resist all evolutionary attempts at reconstruction and any attempt to do away with religious practice as an independent entity or the religious subject as an authentic element in the process of a historical and materialist dialectical system.

The following conclusion can be drawn from these two statements. A theology that is theoretical because it is interested in justification must be apologetical. It cannot simply subordinate itself to the existing types

---

7. For this evolutionary disintegration of the dialectics of liberation, see, for example, J. Habermas's recent attempt to reconstruct historical materialism on the basis of evolution.

of theory if it is to function as theology. If it is theoretical because it is interested in justification, then this theology must be practical and guided by a new dialectical tension between theory and praxis. It can only deal effectively with attempts at evolutionary reconstruction or to impose a total social conditioning of religion by adopting a praxis that breaks open these systems of interpretation. As a theology which seeks to justify, then, fundamental theology is essentially apologetical and practical. It is only in this way that it can guarantee the authenticity of faith and make it valid.[8]

Biblical Defense

We are bound to ask who would really want nowadays to defend Christian hope or the Church. The task has for a long time been regarded with suspicion. Apologetics are thought to be tactically dishonest, dogmatic in the bad sense, tending to take ideological shortcuts and formalistic in argument. The apologist is suspected of being incapable of learning and unwilling to learn, with the result that he reacts with astonishment and firmness to the critical questions that arise spontaneously in new situations.

This practical apologetical aspect of fundamental theology does not, however, mean that the fundamental theologian is necessarily uncritical or insensitive to all theory. On the contrary, it is indicative of a very un-critical attitude to insist exclusively on pure theory (this question will be discussed in greater detail later on). To emphasize the practical apologetical aspect of fundamental theology, then, does not lead to a helpless or impotent opening out of theology or an irrational rigidity and dogmatism toward the current theories. Practical fundamental theology has the difficult task of dealing with these theories in an attempt to demonstrate that they cannot validate their metatheoretical claims to explain away religion or operate with unproved assumptions. The obvious sign of this is the irrational predominance of the symbol of evolution.

The fact that the Christian religion cannot be defended by purely theoretical arguments, but that an apologetical praxis has to be applied in its defense is fully in accordance with the biblical datum of apology. I

---

8. These ideas did not predominate in my article on "Apologetics" in *Sacramentum Mundi I* (Freiburg and London, 1967), 266–76. In that article I maintained that apologetics were neither an adaptation nor an attempt to fit Christian faith into a ready-made, formal and universal pattern, either of a cosmological and metaphysical or of a transcendental, existential, or personal kind. In its justification of faith, it tried to be open to all patterns of faith and to keep what Bonhoeffer had called the "counterlogos" of the cross and resurrection of Jesus Christ constantly in view; this counterlogos could be proved true not as a pure idea, but only in an (historical) activity that was orientated toward its eschatological promises.

would therefore draw attention to two fundamental aspects of this apology within the context of the New Testament which are at the same time concepts of practical reason.

1. It is important to remember that the language of the defense of Christianity that is found in the New Testament is legalistic in origin.[9] Not only the biblical language of this defense, but also such theological concepts as satisfaction, emancipation, autonomy, and so on have their origin in the law. This origin in the language of the law shows that, in the New Testament sense, the Christian is again and again on trial and has in practice to justify his hope in this situation. His defense or apology therefore is a kind of public justification of Christian hope. We know from the history of the early Church that being on trial and speaking in defense of the Christian religion could often be a matter of life or death. A clear example of an early Christian who was both an apologist and a martyr is Justin. This may perhaps justify our claim, despite the fact that it cannot be proved conclusively by linguistic arguments, that defense or apology is very close to what is known in the New Testament as the imitation of Christ.[10] Finally, we are bound to point out that Jesus himself is seen by the evangelists as being in a similar situation of trial. They present us with the encounter that took place between Jesus and his witnesses on the one hand and the political authorities of the state on the other. In and through his suffering and death, Jesus defended his hope.[11]

The biblical concept of defense, then, has a legal origin, even though this usage was not current and it cannot be proved beyond all doubt that apology and imitation are synonymous. This can be expressed in Hasidaean terms in the following way. If an old rabbi were, during one of the bloody persecutions of his people, dragged before the court and asked: "How do you justify your religious praxis?" he would reply: "How can I convince you, if you are not convinced by the suffering of my people?"[12]

2. The biblical concept of apology also has an eschatological and apocalyptic perspective. In the New Testament, what is ultimately involved in this defense is man's trial before Christ in the court of justice at the end of time: "We must all appear before the judgment seat of Christ,

---

9. See G. Ebeling, "Erwägungen zu einer evangelischen Fundamentaltheologie," *Zeitschrift für Theologie und Kirche* 67 (1970). This article contains some important ideas about the theological development of this concept.

10. For the content and meaning of "imitation" in the sense of apologetical praxis, see my *Followers of Christ* (London and New York, 1978).

11. See H. Schlier, *Besinnung auf das Neue Testament* (Freiburg, 1964), 193.

12. The underlying intention of this particular conception of practical fundamental theology is to give valid expression to the inheritance of the Jewish religion which is so often overlooked and to which justice cannot be done in the pure exegesis of Old Testament texts.

so that each one may receive good or evil, according to what he has done in the body" (2 Cor. 5:10). It is obvious that, in this context, the word "apology" can best be translated as "justification."[13] This justification at the end of time will clearly not be a purely intellectual defense of hope, but a praxis. This justification or vindication is, above all, a concept of practical reason.

What, then, does it mean, justification in an eschatological and apocalyptic perspective? Surely any concrete justification is made impossible in advance by the dimensions of this eschatological and apocalyptic perspective, in which the whole of history and human society are visible. Surely too, this gives rise to a dangerous confusion. Is this concept, based as it is on a universal perspective, perhaps not *a priori* unsuitable for the purpose of praxis? Or is it possible, in the present situation in which mankind and the world are placed, for it, because of its universal nature, to be really politically and socially in accordance with that situation? Are there not very many tasks of a universal dimension and on a worldwide scale today which can be described with relative ease, but for which there are apparently no specific subjects of justification, at least not at present?[14]

Outside the Territory of the System

If we take this practical and apologetical aspect of fundamental theology seriously, then the latter will, precisely as a practical fundamental theology, become a political theology of the subject, with certain clear consequences for the theological self-understanding of this discipline. It cannot simply develop as a system of justification without a subject, nor can it provide its themes of its own accord and calculate in advance the difficulty of the challenges or the tests that may confront it. The field in which it proves its value lies outside the territory of any previously conceived theological system. It is, as it were, defined by the social and historical situation with all its painful contradictions. The fundamental theology that I have in mind will always be closely linked to a praxis that is opposed to any attempt to condition religion socially or to reconstruct it theoretically. It is, in other words, linked to the praxis of faith in its mystical and its political dimension.

In this sense, then, fundamental theology is bound to be systematically interrupted by this praxis. This is why it can and should never be a theology that is purely confined to books or lectures — because of its claim to justification. It has to absorb new praxis and new experiences

---

13. See G. Picht, *Wahrheit — Vernunft — Verantwortung* (Stuttgart, 1969), 18–342.
14. Ibid.

if it is to prevent itself from reproducing the concepts of earlier praxis and experiences.

This procedure does not lead automatically to theological continuity. This can only be maintained or acquired by practical fundamental theology if the latter is seen as a corrective with regard to existing theological systems and approaches and if it preserves and passes on the substance and intention of those systems in a critical and corrective relationship with them. What is more, this may also be the way in which we can achieve theological continuity today.[15]

---

15. I am of the opinion that Karl Rahner's transcendental theology can only be continued without a break if it is criticized and corrected with the help of experiences and a praxis that are not derived from the theological system hitherto in use. Rahner's transcendental theology continued to be dramatic and in that respect free of the suspicion of being tautological, as long as it was a corrective, in other words, as long as it was engaged in controversy with a theological opponent. In the initial stages of Rahner's transcendental theology, that opponent was neoscholasticism. The first crises of identity began to appear in Rahner's theology, however, when this opponent finally collapsed in exhaustion in the strong arms of transcendental theology. We may go further and say that even Karl Barth's early *Deus dixit* theology was also a corrective theology. His uncompromising "commitment to God" — with which Barth himself insisted every theology should yet cannot begin — was therefore not a badly concealed positivism of revelation, because it criticized and corrected the predominant liberal theology of the period.

Chapter 7

The Dangerous Memory of
the Freedom of Jesus Christ

The Presence of the Church in Society

The Status of the Theme in Theology and the Church

The question of the presence of the Church in society is ultimately the question of the situation today of theology and the Church as such. The view that this is no more than a question of application or of practical concretization which does not touch the substance of theological truth or the essential being of the Church at all is frequently encountered. This view is, however, in my opinion, a very serious misunderstanding of the situation, both with regard to the position and the task of theology and with regard to the Church itself.

The Situation and Task of Theology

We live in a period when all ideas and concepts, including our concept of God, are determined and deciphered by the criticism of ideology and the sociology of knowledge that have been developed since idealism in accordance with their social interest and historical context. Because of this, it is only possible to make the irreducibility and transcendence of the eschatological message visible and convincing if their critical and liberating power is itself freed from these socially determining factors. Any theology that aims to justify Christian faith and its tradition critically in this way is bound to take this social and practical aspect into account. No such theological theory can allow any abstraction from such problems as public life, justice, and freedom, in other words, political problems. Theology has to be and indeed can be "political" theology and, what is more, it

---

Note: This chapter is an adapted version, rewritten to fit into the whole concept, of a text first prepared in 1970. It was originally given as a paper at the International Congress of theologians in Brussels in September 1970 and was published for the first time in the special number of *Concilium* (1970–71), devoted to that congress, under the title "Zur Präsenz der Kirche in der Gesellschaft."

can be this irrespective of the way in which the political theme should be taken into consideration in determining a Christian's eschatological hope.

With Regard to the Church

It is important to bear in mind here that, as a historical and social reality, the Church is always active as a political factor. In other words, it is political and acts politically before taking up any explicit political position and therefore also before there is any question of criteria governing its present political attitude. The usual supposition that the Church is *a priori* neutral or politically innocent in its attitudes is either uncritical or else it consciously draws a veil over existing political alliances. It is essential to evolve a critical and political form of hermeneutics of the Church if we are to prevent the Church from being uncritically identified with specific political ideologies and thus having it sink to the level of a purely political religion.

That is why "political" theology does not aim to be a regional task of contemporary theology as a whole, but a fundamental task. It does not seek to offer a new sphere of activity to frustrated Christians — that of politics. On the contrary, it tries to carry out the same task that Christian theology has always carried out — that of speaking about God by making the connection between the Christian message and the modern world visible and expressing the Christian tradition in this world as a dangerous memory. In this task, theology cannot simply uncritically ignore the historical distance between the present time and the unrepeatable situation of the biblical testimony, nor can it belittle the importance of that difference. It cannot, in other words, presume that the content and intentions of that testimony are known and simply apply them to the contemporary situation. It has rather to take account of the fact that this historical and social difference again and again raises the question as to what the content and intentions of the biblical testimony really are. In this sense, "political" theology is not simply a theory of the subsequent application of the Christian message, but a theory of the truth of that message with a practical and critical intention for the modern world.

The Theological Basis

The following thesis may serve as a theological basis for our theme: the Church must understand and justify itself as the public witness and bearer of the tradition of a dangerous memory of freedom in the "systems" of our emancipative society. This thesis is based on memory as the fundamental form of expression of Christian faith and on the central and special importance of freedom in that faith. In faith, Christians accomplish the *memoria passionis, mortis et resurrectionis Jesu Christi*. In faith, they remember the testament of Christ's love, in which the kingdom of God appeared among men by initially establishing that kingdom between men, by Jesus' confession of himself as the one who was on the side of the oppressed and rejected and by his proclamation of the coming kingdom of God as the liberating power of unconditional love. This *memoria Jesu Christi* is not a memory which deceptively dispenses Christians from the risks involved in the future. It is not a middle-class counterfigure to hope. On the contrary, it anticipates the future as a future of those who are oppressed, without hope and doomed to fail. It is therefore a dangerous and at the same time liberating memory that oppresses and questions the present because it reminds us not of some open future, but precisely this future, and because it compels Christians constantly to change themselves so that they are able to take this future into account.

This definite memory breaks through the magic circle of the prevailing consciousness. It regards history as something more than a screen for contemporary interests. It mobilizes tradition as a dangerous tradition and therefore as a liberating force in respect of the one-dimensional character and certainty of the one whose "hour is always there" (John 7:6). It gives rise again and again to the suspicion that the plausible structures of a society may be relationships aimed to delude. It also refuses to measure the relevance of its criticism in accordance with what "an elderly, rather sleepy businessman" would regard unquestioningly as relevant "after lunch" and what often functions as a secret criterion for rationality and a sense of reality. Christian faith can and must, in my opinion, be seen in this way as a subversive memory. The Church is, moreover, to some extent the form of its public character. In this sense, the Church's teachings and confessions of faith should be understood as formulae in which this challenging memory is publicly spelled out. The criterion of its authentic Christianity is the liberating and redeeming danger with which it introduces the remembered freedom of Jesus into modern society and the forms of consciousness and praxis in that society.

The Church acts as the public memory of the freedom of Jesus in the systems of our emancipative society. It reminds us of an indebted freedom, God's eschatological history of freedom, which is gained in the cross and resurrection of Jesus and which cannot be absorbed into the ideal of man's coming of age that is contained in the middle-class history of the Enlightenment or into the apotheosis of the history of liberation by revolution. The Church does not dispense us from the responsibility to take care of the history of freedom, but rather initiates us into it: "All things are yours, whether Paul or Apollos or Cephas or the world or life or death or the present or future, all are yours, and you are Christ's and Christ is God's" (1 Cor. 3:21–23). In this sense, then, the Church is an emancipative memory, liberating us from all attempts to idolize cosmic and political powers and make them absolute. In the light of the Church, all political orders appear, in principle, as orders of freedom, and the political ethics of the previously established order are enlarged to include political ethics of radical changes in freedom. Every power of perfection, reconciliation, and peace, which presupposes human freedom and the conflicts involved in it, is reserved in this memory of God.

It is from the memory of this "eschatological reservation" that the Church can and must draw its strength to criticize all totalitarian systems of government and all ideologies of a linear and one-dimensional emancipation. Whenever the history of freedom takes place without reference to this memory of the eschatological reservation, it always seems to fall victim to the compulsive need to substitute a worldly subject for the whole history of freedom, and this always moves in the direction of a totalitarian control of men by men. In the end, a history of freedom which has lost this eschatological memory can only be interpreted as a nondialectical and, to some extent, abstract history of emancipation in which the new conflicts and disasters of the freedom gained are ignored and the idea of coming of age without reserved reconciliation threatens to sink to the level of a commonplace idea of pure survival or cunning animal adaptation.

Where, then, is this eschatological memory of freedom that breaks open our cognitive and operative systems alive? Who brings about those forms of freedom that are so often forgotten or thrust into the background by our emancipative society? One of those forms is the freedom to suffer the suffering of others and to respect the prophecy of others' suffering, even though the negative aspect of suffering seems to be forbidden. Another is the freedom to become old although the public character of old age is denied and even regarded as secretly shameful. There is also the freedom to contemplate, despite the fact that so many people are now hypnotized, in the ultimate stages of their consciousness, by work, performance, and planning. Finally, who will achieve the freedom to make present for us our own questionable and finite nature, even though our public life is open to the suggestion that it will be made even more whole and harmonious? Who will respond to the claim of past sufferings and hopes and the challenge made by those who have died? Who will make men's consciences more sensitive to their claim to justice? Who will cultivate solidarity with those to whom we shall belong in the near future? Who can share his understanding of freedom with those who do not die a heroic death in the frontline of a revolutionary fight for freedom, but will rather die the terribly commonplace death of every day?

Any society that ignores or thrusts into the background these aspects of the history of freedom must pay for this neglect by gradually losing its own visible freedom. The eschaton of that society is boredom. Its myth is a faith in planning. The silent interest of the rationality of that society is to abolish the world as resistance, in order not to continue to experience that world. As Ernst Bloch has said, what we have now "in the West is a patronizing, pluralistic boredom and in the East an imposed oppressed and monolithic boredom.... It looks like a partial eclipse of the sun. Everything is remarkably grey and either the birds do not sing or they sing differently. Something is wrong in any case. The transcending being is weak." Or else the dangerous memory has been extinguished and the eschatological memory has become exhausted.

Has Christianity failed here historically? Has the Church ceased to function historically as the institutional bearer of this Christianity and its memory? Can the future of human freedom be determined only with secular utopias and ideas? All "external" opinions and many of the opinions expressed within the Church would seem to suggest this. In the modern theories of society, the classical criticism of religion has concentrated its attention on the Church. The Church is often described as an organization with a consciousness that is not contemporary. It is thought to impose an institutional taboo on knowledge and productive curiosity. It is regarded as a remnant that is opposed to emancipation. It is thought to have no more than a simulated interest in freedom and the upright progress of man. It has been called an opium in suffering and unjust relationships. According to most modern theories of society, the Church has lost or is rapidly losing its function in contemporary society. In this way, emphatic criticism gives way more and more clearly to indifference or benevolent courtesy, a caricature of the sympathy that is shown to a dying man. Even militant communists are more and more restrained in their struggle against a totally privatized Church. In the vigorous futurologies of the West, the Church has hardly any part to play.

Are the statements made about the Church today in the preceding paragraph simply clichés, expressing one-sided views conditioned by the prevailing systems? Or do they express the fact that the Church is constantly challenged in the world of today, in other words, the suffering situation of the Church of the crucified Lord, which every believer has to take into account?

I am of the opinion that we should not give this theological answer too quickly, because it fails to take into consideration a profound aspect of the prevailing attitude in criticism of the Church. This is man's historical experience with the Church, his collective memory of disappointments caused by the Church, the historical conscience of generations who are aware of the Church's dubious alliances with the power structures of society and the frequent impression of imbalance in the Church as representing a religion that is not believed, but is constantly replacing itself. This memory has to be taken into consideration. It is much more difficult to efface than is often assumed. It is indeed the most pressing historical and hermeneutical problem confronting contemporary ecclesiology and far more important than, for example, that of finding historical evidence for the foundation of the Church and the apostolic succession. This problem cannot, moreover, be solved by providing a better or more subtle interpretation of the Church's past history. It can only be solved by a painful process of change involving proof of the spirit and strength of a new praxis.

The roots of the ethics of the reform of the Church are to be found here.[1] These ethics are concerned not with modern attitudes that uncritically accept the prevailing illusions of contemporary society, but with the fundamental question of the historical identity and continuity of the Church and its mission. Church in this instance means above all: we Christians who try to live in the memory of Christ and for whom the idea of a tradition of this memory which is completely free of the Church as an institution and which entrusts this memory exclusively to the private individual is an illusion.

Options with a Practical and Critical Intention

I would therefore like to make at least three suggestions here with a practical and critical intention.

a. An important question in this context is that of spirituality and the formation of spirituality in the Church as a spirituality of liberated freedom which bears witness to and justifies in the extension of a freedom that is critical of society. The witness borne by this freedom will have characteristics that differ according to the different spheres of society. The forms of freedom that will be required and practiced in the systems of the prosperous societies of the West will be those forms which I have already mentioned: namely, those that have been largely forgotten or thrust into the background. In the systems of the southern regions, the witness borne by this freedom will take the form above all of a courageous struggle against social misery. In these regions, too, there will inevitably be striking evidence of the interference of this testimony to freedom in the sphere of politics. In this situation, it would be objectively dishonest to appeal to

---

1. See J. B. Metz, *Reform und Gegenreformation heute* (Mainz, 1969); Metz, *Followers of Christ.*

the great variety of interpretations of political realities as a justification of the Church's failure to take up a position in politics. Bishops and theologians can easily become mandarins in a Church that continues to practice the same unchanging form of integralism and to establish political alliances under cover of its traditional neutrality and political innocence without regard for the actual suffering and real oppression that exist in society.

The freedom which is critical of society and which bears witness to itself in the spirituality of liberated freedom is never purely intellectual in its attitude. Its criticism has none of the characteristics of "total" criticism. It suffers from the pain of self-denial, persistence, impatience, and patience — these are characteristics demanded by the Christian memory of freedom as an imitation of Christ. Because of this, it is not simply a copy of the prevailing criticism of society. It cannot moreover simply be thrust into the alternative of prayer and action. It tries to gain from prayer the freedom that it needs from the plausible structures of social mechanisms and prejudices and the strength to be independent enough to take liberating action in the interest of others, the "least of the brethren." In this action, moreover, prayer can set itself free from the suspicion that it is no more than an opium of the people and that God's name is invoked simply to soften the anonymous fate that again and again befalls every human hope of freedom. The spirituality of liberated freedom cannot therefore be limited to a pure experience of cult that is isolated and free from all the conflicts, repressions, and challenges of everyday life. This way to a purely cultic spirituality is often recommended today and it would certainly seem to be an objective need in the middle class. All the same, it is a wrong way. At the end of it is the esoteric Church, the opium of the intellectuals.

The spirituality of liberated freedom that is required here increases in strength as our willingness to suffer the sufferings of others grows. It also increases as men have a conscience not only about what they do or do not do to others, but also about what they let happen to others and as they cease to regard, in accordance with the rules of the society of exchange, only those who are of a like mind as their brethren and to treat all others as an anonymous mass. Only those who are cynically dedicated to power will dismiss these aspects of socially critical freedom as romantic.

Is the question of this one indivisible freedom not always associated with those impotent people who lack the power that presupposes the power of love and whose only ally is the dangerous memory of the hope of freedom? The Church should support the institutionalized, authoritative interest of this freedom and indeed be that interest in season and out of season, because of the radical threats and catastrophes that have punctuated the history of freedom. In this attempt, the witness borne by the Church to liberated freedom can only acquire authority (from religious competence!) if it remains linked to the interest of a love looking for its own way through history in the track of others' suffering. It is only when the Church listens to the prophecy of this suffering, poverty, and oppression that it will truly listen to the word of Christ and that it will be, as the visible Church, at the same time the invisible Church of the Spirit of Christ. To achieve this, it will have to conquer new fields of testimony and acquire new forms of charisma to express this liberated freedom.

b. It is important that the processes within the Church leading to a critical public life, a transition from an emphatic to a constitutional freedom and a real culture of freedom in the Church, should be encouraged and promoted as courageously and constructively as possible. Critical freedom in the Church cannot be measured against purely psychological or sociological themes or allowed to solidify into a jargon of helpless protest. The radical question that confronts the Church today is whether it is prepared to live with the conflicts arising from critical freedom and whether it can understand those problems as an aspect of itself. This is not simply a claim made by a small elite group of intellectuals in the Church, but a fundamental question for the people of the Church as a whole. It is, after all, not the critical intellectuals who will be a problem in the Church, so much as the so-called simple faithful who even now seem to be profoundly irritated, not so much by a critical theology as by the institution of the Church itself. It is the change in the Church that has given rise to confusion and crises of identity.

The frequently mentioned confusion among the members of the Church has come about because they have been exposed to change in an unloving and authoritarian way by the Church and yet have not been provided with a critical understanding of the reformability of the Church itself. How is it possible for the "simple faithful" to continue to grasp the identity of the one Church in all its changes and for them not to feel that they have been deceived if they lack the critical appreciation of their Church that would enable them to perceive the continuity in the changes and to know that a process of change is an essential part of the historical identity of this one *ecclesia semper reformanda?* One of the causes of the crisis in the Church today is not that there is too much criticism, but rather that there is a catastrophic absence of fundamental and practiced critical freedom in the Church. This absence of critical freedom has, moreover, made the simple faithful the focal point of crisis in the Church of tomorrow. The silent majority in the Church forms a very problematical body. The crisis of religious identity among the simple faithful should therefore not be underestimated. Who will, in the end, save himself from a dangerous indifferentism or a skeptical form of resignation, through which increasingly firm and fatal lines are being drawn between the Church as an institution and Christian people?

However much it is stressed that the Church is the people of God and the universal priesthood of all believers and however much emphasis is placed on the importance of laypeople in the Church, the number of those who really feel themselves to be Church is nevertheless becoming smaller and smaller. Where a collective identification is impossible, there is always a danger of panic. If we blame those who have difficulties of identification for this situation and appeal prematurely to the Church as a "little flock," the only way ahead that we shall be able to point out to the Church is the way to sectarianism.

c. I would therefore like to suggest that the third task confronting us is to prevent Christians from developing an increasingly sectarian attitude. The situation in the Church is alarming. Its increasing cognitive isolation in a world which it has no more influence to define threatens to drive it into a closed sectarian attitude or else to make it adapt itself in a modernistic way. There is obviously a danger that the Christian message will be completely adapted and Church Christianity will sink to the level of an unnecessary religious paraphrase of modern processes in the world. Over and against this danger that the Church will lose itself by a process of active adaptation there is the danger of loss through passive adaptation. The latter danger is far less in the foreground of our attention today than it would be if we were really concerned with the way that the Church should follow in society now and in the future. This danger is that the Church will become a sect in the theological sense. In other words, it is the danger of a traditional sectarian orthodoxy and a sectarian attitude in a closed Church.

The symptoms of an increasingly sectarian attitude would seem to be a noncreative preservation of traditions, in other words, a pure traditionalism, a growing inability or unwillingness to have new experiences and to apply them critically to a self-understanding of the Church and its constitutions and documents. Many aspects of the continuing controversy between Christian confessions are, in my opinion, sectarian, as are the zealotic language and the new militant behavior in the controversies within the Church itself. In other words, active Church life is being transformed into a joyless and humorless zealotism.

The Church, as the Church of the Son, cannot, however, remain closed to the "strangers" in the historical world that it does not understand and expect to preserve itself in that closed state. This "conditioning by strangers" is not something that was subsequently added to the Church. On the contrary, it is an element of the Church's constitution and part of its *specificum christianum*. The Church cannot, in other words, know in advance and without historical experience and debate both what is human and what is Christian in the full sense of the word. If this is forgotten in the Church, then there is a danger that the Church will become a sect in the theological sense.

This warning of the danger of sectarianism is not made in ignorance of the fact that the Church is increasingly becoming a minority in society as a whole now and in the future. The Church could not be defined as a sect in the theological sense simply because it is a minority. It could only be called a sect because of its attitude. It need not fear being a minority, nor need it be ashamed of that status, unless it came to regard itself as the institution that brought about the history of liberated freedom in the world and thus misunderstood itself so completely that it thought of itself as an ideology that replaced its own hope of freedom. The minority status of the Church may even be a positive opportunity, giving it greater mobility, bringing it closer to the oppressed and overlooked minorities in society and taking it out of its parapolitical structures. It may in this way become, in the strict sense of the word, a purgatory, with the result that the freedom of Jesus himself, the dangerous memory of which is indispensable to the future of freedom as such, may be represented in a renewed and more vigorous way in the Church's life.

Chapter 8

A Short Apology of Narrative

Contemporary theological dictionaries are in some ways unreliable because they leave out so much — for example, the word "story" or "narrative." I should like, in this chapter, to write a short apology of narrative, especially since the category of "dangerous memory," which I used in a previous article in Concilium[1] to throw light on the understanding of Christian faith in our present situation clearly has a narrative structure.[2]

I cannot hope to deal systematically or fully here with the theological theme of narrative, but can only mention a number of different and significant points.[3] I have not attempted a linguistic analysis partly because I am simply not competent to do so. Another reason is because it is not theologically relevant to incorporate the narrative potential of Christianity into a linguistic theory (in order to close it as a form of prescientific communication). An even more important reason is that narrative processes have to be protected, interrupted in order to justify them critically, and even guided in the direction of a competent narrative without allowing the experience of faith to be silenced like every original experience.

Narrative and Experience

"However familiar we may be with the name, the narrator is not present for us, alive and active. Not only is he remote from us — he is always becoming more remote. It is as though an apparently inalienable and assured ability had been taken away from us. This is the ability to exchange experiences."[4] The atrophy of narrative is particularly dangerous in theology. If the category of narrative is lost or outlawed by theology as precritical, then real or original experiences of faith may come to lack objectivity

---

1. "The Future in the Memory of Suffering," *Concilium* 76 (June 1972).

2. I have discussed this in greater detail in my article "Erinnerung," in *Handbuch Philosophischer Grundebegriffe*, vol. 1, ed. H. Krings, H. M. Baumgartner, and C. Wild (Munich, 1973).

3. I have dealt with the significance of a memorative and narrative soteriology for the central theme of the history of redemption and freedom in "Erlösung und Emanzipation," *Stimmen der Zeit* 98 (1973).

4. W. Benjamin, "Der Erzähler," *Illuminationen* (Frankfurt, 1961), 409.

102

and become silenced, and all linguistic expressions of faith may therefore be seen as categorical objectivizations or as changing symbols of what cannot be said) In this way, the experience of faith will become vague and its content will be preserved only in ritual and dogmatic language, without the narrative form showing any power to exchange experience.

Theology is, above all, concerned with direct experiences expressed in narrative language. This is clear throughout scripture, from the beginning, the story of creation, to the end, where a vision of the new heaven and the new earth is revealed. All this is disclosed in narrative. The world created from nothing, man made from the dust, the new kingdom proclaimed by Jesus, himself the new man, resurrection as a passage through death to life, the end as a new beginning, the life of future glory — all these show that reasoning is not the original form of theological expression, which is above all that of narrative.(The *logos* of theology, so long as it conceals its own narrative form, is as embarrassed by them as reason is by questions concerning the beginning and the end and the destiny of what is new and has never yet been) The question about the beginning, the *arche*, which enabled the Greeks with their *logos* to break the spell of pure narrative in myth, leads thought straight back to narrative. The beginning and the end can only be discussed in narrative form. Kant was aware of this when he spoke of the "rhapsodic beginning of thought" which was not open to argumentative reconstruction. Above all, what is new and has never yet been can only be introduced in narrative. As Adorno has observed in the closing passages of his *Minima Moralia*, if reason is closed to the narrative exchange of experiences of what is new and completely breaks off that exchange for the sake of its own critical nature and its autonomy, it will inevitably exhaust itself in reconstructions and become no more than a technique. This question will be discussed more fully below.

[margin handwriting: logos = reason or structure]

The Practical and Performative Aspect of Narrative

There are examples of narrative traditions which resist the influence of our supposedly postnarrative age — for instance, the Hasidic stories, Johann Peter Hebel's or Bertolt Brecht's "calendar" stories, or the "traces" of Ernst Bloch, whose main work, *Das Prinzip Hoffnung*, reads like a great encyclopedia of "hope" stories. They all illustrate the practical character of such narratives, their communication of an experience and close involvement of the narrator and the listener in the experience narrated.

> Most born story-tellers pursue a practical interest. . . . This is indicative of the distinctive nature of all true stories, all of which have

an overt or hidden use — a moral, a practical instruction, a rule of life. In every case, the story-teller is a man who knows what to do with the listener.... His stories are based on experience, either his own or other people's, which he transforms into the experience of those who listen to his stories.[5]

Martin Buber has reaffirmed this characteristic in his introduction to the Hasidic stories and has also drawn attention to other important features of the narrative form:

> The story is itself an event and has the quality of a sacred action. ...It is more than a reflection — the sacred essence to which it bears witness continues to live in it. The wonder that is narrated becomes powerful once more.... A rabbi, whose grandfather had been a pupil of Baal Shem Tov, was once asked to tell a story. "A story ought to be told," he said, "so that it is itself a help," and his story was this. "My grandfather was paralyzed. Once he was asked to tell a story about his teacher and he told how the holy Baal Shem Tov used to jump and dance when he was praying. My grandfather stood up while telling the story and the story carried him away so much that he had to jump and dance to show how the master had done it. From that moment, he was healed. This is how stories ought to be told."[6]

This text is remarkable for two reasons. In the first place, it is a successful example in a critical, postnarrative age of how narrative teaching can be linked with narrative self-enlightenment about the very interest which underlies the narrative process. In this case, the story is not ideologically unconscious of the interest that governs it. It presents this interest and "tries it out" in the narrative process. It verifies or falsifies itself and does not simply leave this to discussion about the story which lies outside the narrative process. This is, in my opinion, a very important aspect of the narrative form which cannot, unfortunately, be pursued further here.

In the second place, Buber's text points to an inner relationship between story and sacrament, in other words, to the story as an effective sign and to the narrative aspect of the sacrament as a sign. The sacramental sign can easily be characterized as a "linguistic action" in which the unity of the story as an effective word and as practical effect is expressed in the same process. The aspect of ceremony and ritual may perhaps mean that the sacrament is not clearly recognized as a saving narrative. On closer inspection, however, it is evident first that the linguistic formulae used

---

5. Ibid., 412ff.
6. M. Buber, *Werke* 3 (Munich, 1963), 71.

in the administration of the sacraments are typical examples of what are known as "performative" expressions,[7] and second that they narrate something. The story form occurs, for instance, in the eucharistic prayer ("on the night that he was betrayed . . . ") and the formula of the sacrament of penance is incorporated within the framework of a narrative action.

I am convinced that it is very important to bring out this narrative aspect of the sacrament more clearly. If this is done, the relationship between word and sacrament may be more fully elaborated theologically. Above all, it should also be possible to relate the sacramental action more closely to stories of life and suffering and to reveal it as a saving narrative.

The Pastoral and Social Aspect of Narrative

Marginal groups and religious sects are always active in society and it would be wrong for the churches *a priori* to silence or reject their disturbing message. Although the underlying ambiguity of the Jesus People, for example, prevents us from accepting them uncritically as providing the best chance of Christian renewal, they have one very positive merit — they and others employ not argument and reasoning but narrative. They tell the story of their conversion and retell biblical stories, sometimes in a patently helpless way that is open to manipulation. Is this simply a sign of spiritual regression, of the danger of archaism or infantilism in the religious life, of emotional, pseudoreligious enthusiasm, or of an arbitrary and contemptuous rejection of serious theological reasoning? Or is it rather the visible appearance of something that is usually repressed in the public and official life of the churches? Are these marginal groups not in fact drawing on something that has for too long been hidden and neglected in Christianity, its narrative potential? Are they not remembering that Christians do not primarily form an argumentative and reasoning community, but a storytelling community and that the exchange of experiences of faith, like that of any "new" experience, takes a narrative form? Finally, does this not apply above all to the marginal groups which, in their refusal to speak the language of ritual and theology, are almost silent?

This is important in the question of pastoral care and the proclamation of faith, which are, I believe, in a critical situation because we are no longer able to narrate with a practical and socially critical effect and with a dangerous and liberating intention. For too long, we have tried to suppress the narrative potential of Christianity and have confined it to credulous children and old people, although it is these who are especially sensitive to false or substitute stories or to an illusory exchange

---

7. See J. L. Austin, *How to Do Things with Words* (Cambridge, Mass., 1962).

of experiences.) This is why, in giving renewed emphasis to narrative, it
is important to avoid the possible misunderstanding that "storytelling"
preachers and teachers will be justified in their narration of anecdotes,
when what is required are arguments and reasoning. After all, there is
a time for storytelling and a time for argument. There is a difference
between the two which has to be recognized.

A second misunderstanding has also to be avoided, that of believing that to stress the narrative element in pastoral care, preaching, and
teaching is to withdraw into the purely private sphere or the aesthetic
sphere of good taste. If they give this impression, our stories will only
reveal the extent to which we have forgotten how to tell them. It is true
that there are many different kinds of narrative — stories which pacify,
those which relieve feelings, like political jokes made under a dictator-
ship, and those which conceal a quest for freedom and stir the listener to
imitation. Stories are told by very wise men who have, as Heinrich von
Kleist observed, "eaten a second time of the tree of knowledge" and by
little people who are oppressed or have not yet come of age. These, however, tell not only stories which tempt them to celebrate their immature
dependence or their oppressed state, but also stories which are dangerous and which seek freedom.(Freedom and enlightenment, the transition
from dependence to coming of age, are not achieved simply by giving
up narrative language in favor of the art of reasoning possessed by those
who are enlightened and those who claim it as their privilege.)(The old
problem of the relationship between intellectuals and the working classes
has, I believe, its origins primarily in a misunderstanding among intellectuals of the emancipatory character of narrative language, just as the
value of the narrative form which is at the basis of Christianity is so
often underestimated by theologians.)

There can, of course, be no *a priori* proof of the critical and liberating
effect of such stories, which have to be encountered, listened to, and
told again. But surely there are, in our postnarrative age, storytellers
who can demonstrate what "stories" might be today — not just artificial,
private constructions, but narratives with a stimulating effect and aiming
at social criticism, "dangerous" stories in other words. Can we perhaps
retell the Jesus stories nowadays in this way?

The Theological Aspect of Narrative —
Narrative as the Medium of Salvation and History

The emphasis given in the preceding section to the pastoral aspect of the
story form might give the impression that narrative is above all useful in
teaching and catechesis as an indispensable aid to applied theology, but

that it does not affect the structure of theology itself in any way. This is, of course, not the intention at all — to say that the narrative form characterizes the proclamation of faith and rational argument theology is too superficial a distinction, suppressing the underlying structure of theology itself. In this section, then, the theological aspect of narrative and the inseparable connection between narrative and argument (explanation, analysis, and so on) will be discussed. The categories used in this section, including that of a narrative history of suffering, will be discussed in greater detail below.

The question as to how history and salvation can be related without each being diminished may be regarded as of central importance in contemporary theology. History is the experience of reality in conflict and contradiction, whereas salvation is, theologically speaking, their reconciliation by the act of God in Jesus Christ. An integral part of history is the suffering experience of non-identity through violence and oppression, injustice and inequality, guilt, finiteness, and death. In this sense, history is always a history of suffering. (When all men enjoy, as they do now, equal opportunities in a classless society, it should not be difficult to regard history as a history of suffering, since it is precisely in such a period that man's self-destructive nihilism, his despair and boredom — what Ernst Bloch has called the "melancholy of fulfillment" — often becomes so apparent.)

Can the theology of salvation and of man's redemption and reconciliation through Jesus Christ really hold its own against this history of suffering and the non-identity of history? Does it not *a priori* avoid the suffering of historical non-identity and lead an unhistorical and therefore mythological existence above the heads of men who are humiliated and even destroyed by the burden of their own history of suffering? Does the accumulated suffering of history not result in theology becoming cynical toward history? Is there perhaps a theological mediation between salvation and history which has only been taken seriously as a history of suffering? Can this theological mediation exist without becoming reconciled in too ambitious and ultimately too speculative and too self-deceiving a way with this history of suffering or without salvation-history being suspended in view of this history of suffering? With variants, this is the central question of systematic theology today and I believe that purely rational theological arguments cannot provide an answer to it. I should like at this point to clarify this statement by referring to the solutions to this problem which have been suggested by modern theology.[8]

---

8. I have considered the relationship between salvation and history in some detail in the medium of man's history of suffering in my article mentioned in n. 3 above.

The first of these solutions can be described as the existential and transcendental interpretation of the relationship between salvation and history. The question here is whether salvation and history are not reconciled by an existential or transcendental reduction of history to "historicity" and by a withdrawal from the non-identity of history to a mysterious identity of existence or of the subject which cannot be expressed.

A second solution suggests that salvation is conditioned by the history of suffering, projected into the future and, out of respect for the non-identity of history as a history of suffering, kept — so to speak — at stake. One question which arises again and again in connection with this solution, however, is whether a salvation which is always at stake is in any way different from a saving utopia, of which only heuristic use can be made in the history of human freedom.

A third solution has been received with interest in the German-speaking countries especially and merits rather more detailed discussion. A connection between the history of salvation and that of suffering is to be found in referring this question back to the central question of the specifically Christian understanding of God, in other words, by reference to the theme of the Trinity. The non-identity of the history of suffering can therefore, with God's *kenosis* in Jesus' crucifixion in mind, be included in the trinitarian history of God, so that, as Moltmann has observed, suffering becomes "suffering between God and God."

This solution has been suggested by certain Protestant theologians following Karl Barth, especially E. Jüngel, and J. Moltmann in his book on the crucified God, and by Catholics following Karl Rahner's proposals regarding the unity of the immanent Trinity. Among the latter, H. Küng has touched on this question of the historicity of God in his interpretation of Hegel's Christology and H. Urs von Balthasar has dealt with it penetratingly in his interpretation of the paschal mystery within the sphere of God's *kenosis* history understood in the trinitarian sense.

In view of these attempts to solve the problem, I should like to express a fundamental consideration here. The non-identity of the history of suffering cannot be canceled out in a dialectical process of the trinitarian history of salvation in such a way that it preserves its historical character. This is because this non-identity is not the same as the negativity of the dialectical process. In any attempt to interpret the division in the history of man's suffering within this dialectical process, an exchange will take place between the negativity of suffering and the negativity of the dialectical concept of suffering. A purely conceptual reconciliation between the history of salvation as the expression of the history of the redemption accomplished in Jesus Christ and the history of man's suffering is, in my opinion, not possible, because it can only lead either to a dualistic gnostic perpetuation of suffering in God or to a reduction of suffering to the level of a concept. This dilemma cannot be resolved by any more subtle speculative reasoning. It can only be resolved if salvation and redemption in the non-identity of the history of suffering are approached in a different way.

This brings me to the formulation of the following thesis. A theology of salvation which neither conditions nor suspends the history of salvation nor ignores the non-identity of the history of suffering cannot be purely argumentative. It must also be narrative. It is fundamentally a memorative and narrative theology. A narrative memory of salvation would in no sense lead to a regressive confusion of the distinction that dominates our problem. On the contrary, it would enable salvation in history, which is, of course, a history of suffering, to be expressed without either salvation or history being diminished. The category of narrative memory both prevents salvation and redemption from becoming paradoxically unhistorical and subordinates them to the logical identity of dialectical mediation.

Narrative is unpretentious in its effect. It does not have, even from God, the dialectical key which will open every door and throw light on the dark passages of history before they have been trodden. It is not, however, without light itself. Pascal drew attention to this light in distinguishing, in his *Memorial*, between the narrated "God of Abraham, Isaac and Jacob" and the God of rational argument, the "God of the philosophers."

This narrative memory of salvation is, above all, not a purely ad hoc construction designed to solve our problem. It goes much deeper than this, making present the mediation of the history both of salvation and of man's suffering as encountered in the testaments of our faith. If this narrative memory is reduced by theology to a preliminary mythological stage in the Christian *logos*, then theology is clearly functioning uncritically with regard to the possibilities and the limits of expressing the Christian message positively in the experience of the non-identity of history.

It is often forgotten, in the theological criticism of mythology, that the narration of critical argument is inherent in theology as a mediating aspect of its content. This also has to be borne in mind in connection with historical criticism in theology. Without anticipating the content of the following section too much, it is important to point out here that there is a difference between regarding the historical question and the historical truth that is related to it as a problem that has been forced on Christianity in modern times and is therefore in this sense inevitable and as a medium in which the truth of Christianity and its saving message are originally expressed and identified. A purely argumentative theology which conceals its origin and does not make this present again and again in narrative memory inevitably leads, in the history of human suffering, to those many modifications in reasoning which result in the extinction of the identifiable content of Christian salvation. I do not intend this to be regarded as a reason for excluding argument from theology. There is no question of regressively obscuring the distinction between narrative memory and theological argument. It is much more a question of acknowledging the relative value of rational argument, the primary function of which is to protect the narrative memory of salvation in a scientific world, to allow it to be at stake and to prepare the way for a renewal of this narrative, without which the experience of salvation is silenced.

The Narrative Structure of Critical Reason

Does what I have suggested so far not amount ultimately to an uncritical blurring of differences in view of the modern emphasis on critical reason? Is the idea of a history of human suffering not made arbitrary and unsuitable by modern historical criticism? How can narrative and criticism be reconciled with each other?

As a result of the triumph of historicism, all tradition, including the narrative and memorative tradition of Christianity, has been transformed into history, that is, into the object of a critical reconstruction of historical reason. As G. Krüger pointed out, the relationship between historical criticism and the past "not only presupposes that this past is past, but also clearly aims to strengthen and affirm this absence of present reality in what was in the past. History has taken the place of tradition and this means that it occupies that place."[9] Since this was written, a criticism of this historical reasoning has been developed which does not accept without question the absence of memory and of tradition in the scientific world of today, the absence which has resulted from our preoccupation with historicism. This criticism has, above all, been developed in the context of modern hermeneutics and also of a practical and critical philosophy of history and society which is especially indebted to the practical philosophy of Kant and his successors and to the modern criticism of ideology, including the neo-Marxist and the psychoanalytical varieties of this.[10]

---

9. G. Krüger, "Die Bedeutung der Tradition für die philosophische Forschung," *Studium Generale* 4 (1951): 322ff.

10. A detailed discussion of the whole question outlined in this section will be found in my article, "Erinnerung," mentioned in n. 2 above.

This criticism, which is based on the distinction between Moltmann's "knowledge and interest," is concerned with the fundamental themes of historical reason, with the "criticism of criticism" and with the need to expose the abstract will to criticism as an ideology which unquestioningly gives way to a supposed progress in the critical consciousness. This "criticism of criticism" is not a purely formal metacriticism which transposes the problem on to a purely theoretical plane. It deals rather with the problem as one of practical reason which occurs within certain historical memorative and narrative traditions. In this sense, history is — not as reconstructed history, but as memorative and narrative traditions — immanent in reason, which, in this criticism, becomes practical reason. The theme of narrative memory inevitably occurs again and again in this context and, what is more, it is in this case critical with regard to historical reason, which itself becomes more and more a technology looking back at the past and finally a "history" processed into a data bank, a computer memory without narrative and unable either to remember or to forget.

As Theodor Adorno observed, "Forgetting is inhuman because man's accumulated suffering is forgotten — the historical trace of things, words, colors and sounds is always the trace of past suffering. This is why tradition is nowadays confronted with an insoluble contradiction. It is not present and cannot be evoked, but as soon as all tradition is extinguished, inhumanity begins."

Anyone who does not accept this almost insoluble difficulty will inevitably insist that there must be renewed respect for the history of man's suffering in our critical consciousness. This intention will only strike critical reason as obsolete if this respect for the history of suffering is denied because of a fear of heteronomy and if the authority of those who suffer is consequently destroyed in the interest of an abstract autonomy of reason. Whenever this respect is, however, preserved, then reason becomes in a sense "perceptive" in a way that cannot be expressed in the usual contrast which is made between authority and knowledge and which forms the most common framework for any discussion of the problem of the autonomy of reason. In this perception, history, as a remembered history of suffering, acquires for reason the form of a "dangerous tradition," which is passed on not in a purely argumentative manner, but as narrative, that is, in "dangerous stories."

These dangerous stories break through the spell of a historical reconstruction based on abstract reason and repudiate any attempt to reconstruct man's consciousness from the abstract unity of "I think." Above all, they show that man's consciousness is a consciousness which is "entwined in stories," which always has to rely on narrative identification and which, when the relative importance of the magisterium

of history has been recognized, cannot entirely do without the magisterium of stories. In his film *Fahrenheit 451* François Truffaut presented
in a most vivid form this "consciousness in stories," which is nourished
by the accumulated narrative potential that is derived from books, as a
refuge of resistance: the only alternative to a world of total manipulation
and absence of freedom.

Some Questions in Conclusion

I should like to conclude by asking a number of questions that arise in
connection with this short apology of narrative. How, for example, can
the term *narrative* or *story* be defined more precisely? It cannot, after
all, be regarded as synonymous with the term *historical account*, since
nonhistorical forms of knowledge or communication, such as the saga,
fairytale, or legend, have a narrative structure. What is the relationship
between fiction and authenticity in narrative texts? What does it mean
when we say that a story is "true" and in what sense can we speak
of a narrative disclosure of truth? What relationship is there between
narrated time and physical time? How are the story and the storyteller
related to each other and how does the difference between the story
and the storyteller prevent us from regarding narration as a pure textual
problem?

   In connection with the undoubted presence of narrative aspects in the
individual sciences, we are bound to ask whether these are of merely secondary importance and of purely heuristic value. Do change, continuity,
and discontinuity in the sciences and in examples of narrative form have
to be made explicit in logic? Does our insistence on the narrative structure of theology not give rise to renewed questions about the scientific
nature of theology and the cognitive character and the binding force of
theological propositions?

   Finally, among other questions, there is that of the historical Jesus —
how are the history of Jesus and the stories of Jesus related? Has the
canon of the Old and New Testaments not caused a "ban" to be imposed
on narrative, preventing a retelling or further telling of stories in accordance with the contemporary situation? And should the meaning of the
distinction between canonical and apocryphal stories not be reexamined?

Chapter 9

An Identity Crisis in Christianity?

Transcendental and Political Responses

My topic concerning the identity crisis of Christianity provides me with the opportunity for sketching some representative positions in contemporary German and Middle-European systematic theology, namely transcendental theology, universal-historical theology, and political theology. In doing this, I am fully aware of the fact that the future of European theology is no longer what it used to be.

My reflections imply a criticism of Karl Rahner's transcendental theology. But this criticism is profoundly inspired by my admiration and gratitude to my mentor and close personal friend, Karl Rahner. From him one can learn even while criticizing him. Probably this kind of criticism is a better way of remaining faithful to his intentions. Theological loyalty has its own dialectics!

Identity Crisis:
Symptoms and Nontheological Theories

There are symptoms and theories of a historical crisis of identity in Christianity. Almost all the theories which seek to explain the structures and tendencies of the present age are implicitly theories about this crisis. For example, the neo-Marxist theory which affirms the utopian content of Christianity but denies its strictly religious character; the theories of culture in Western middle-class societies on the basis of a logic of evolution which affirms the functions of religion in the development of culture but once again denies its indispensability; theories about the historical discontinuity of Christianity and the modern age; theories about the widespread but mostly unnoticed atrophy of the religious consciousness itself in our times; theories about the Christian churches as "cognitive minorities," and so on.

These nontheological and non-Christian theories about the historical crisis or even demise of Christianity are reflected in the minds of Christians and in the life of the churches. Not only Christian intellectuals, but

believers in general (and this is, of course, much more alarming) are beset by more and more doubts and anxieties. Is it not possible, at least in
central Europe, to observe for the first time perhaps a widespread disappearance of inner and intense convictions about faith? Is there not, at
all levels of society, an inability not only to be sorrowful, but also to be
consoled? Is this inability not increasing? Is consolation not understood
except as an impotent form of pacification? These symptoms and others
that are related to them in the heart of Christian life today would seem
to point to the real existence of a crisis of identity in Christianity of the
kind that has already been established in theory.

How does theology understand the historical identity of Christianity
in face of this situation?

Theological Theories about the Present Situation of Christianity: A Spectrum of Positions

I give to those theological theories about the present situation of Christianity that have been elaborated in argument and are therefore effective
from the theological point of view the rather cursory description of
transcendental and *idealistic* theories. This title therefore includes such
different approaches as the universal-historical and the transcendental
approaches. If I am lacking in consideration in my generalized description of these approaches, it is because I want to clarify in as few
words as possible the intention underlying the postidealistic narrative
and practical-political approach of political theology.

Among the *universal-historical* approaches that are described (critically) here as "idealistic" is not only Wolfhart Pannenberg's influential
ontology of history and meaning which is strongly orientated toward
Hegel and in which the idea of a meaning of history is not a category of
practical reason, but (following idealistic traditions) a category of reflection. A universally historical and idealistic conception — in the sense of
a stage in the history of human freedom that can be eschatologically and
messianically integrated into Christianity — has also been provided by
Jürgen Moltmann, in his impressive attempt to interpret the present situation of Christianity in the light of the revolutionary history of freedom.
Theories of Christianity based on liberal tradition can also be regarded,
for different reasons, as belonging to this approach. Despite all their individual differences, however, these theories have one thing in common:
they all pay careful attention to history as the place where the crisis of
identity has occurred in Christianity.

As opposed to this first group of theories, there is one consistently
elaborated theological theory of the present situation of Christianity in

the Catholic world (which has an influence far beyond Catholicism). This is the *transcendental theory* of *anonymous Christianity* as developed by Karl Rahner. In describing this theory as a transcendental and idealistic concept, I take as my point of departure a practical fundamental theology which understands itself as political theology. This postidealistic theology is characterized by the cognitive primacy of praxis, that is, by the dialectics of theory and praxis. This praxis is basically political because there is no individual moral praxis which is politically innocent. For this postidealistic theology the notion of God is basically a practical and political notion: God cannot be thought of at all unless this idea irritates and encroaches on the immediate interests of the subjects who are trying to think of it. Thinking about God is a review of interests and needs that are directly related to ourselves. Conversion, metanoia, and exodus are not simply moral or educative categories — they are also and above all noetic categories. Stories of conversion and memories of exodus are therefore not simply dramatic embellishments of a previously conceived "pure" theology. On the contrary, they form part of the basic structure of this theology. This practical-political structure of the idea of God is the reason why the concept of God is basically narrative and memorative (as well as the concept of truth). But let us return to Rahner!

The theory of anonymous Christianity sees the historical crisis of identity in the form of the dilemma that arises on the one hand from the increasingly obvious social particularity of the Church and on the other from the universal nature of the Church's mission and of God's saving will as represented in the Church. This theory seems to me to be dominated both by the central theological idea of God's free and universal will to save and by human respect for the hidden depths of man's existence, which is not open to absolute reflection and within which man is always to some extent anonymous even to himself. In his theory of anonymous Christianity, Rahner has only extrapolated his transcendental view of man as the being who has been withdrawn from himself into God or as the being who is "condemned to transcendence," who is "always already with God," even in every act of denial of God, and whose freedom consists (only) in accepting this being (in faith) or in suppressing it (in lack of faith). In his reflective articulation of this freedom, man has to take into account dissonances and even contradictions between what is explicitly said and what is done in fact, between acts of freedom and reflective self-assurance and so on. It would, of course, be impossible to examine here Rahner's profound and highly developed theory of transcendental faith, which is obviously based on an idealistic theory of knowledge and on the traditional doctrine *fides implicita* and *bona fides*. All that I can do here is to point to the result of this approach when it is applied to a theological theory about the present situation of Christianity. Nowadays, the Church is no longer able to reach a great number of people and is bound to take seriously into account that it will not be able, in the future, to make many people and groups of people explicitly Christian. This means that, according to Rahner's theory, the salvation of these people can be seen by the Church as possible in an anonymous form of Christianity.

The Transcendental Theory of Anonymous Christianity: A Few Questions, Not Yet a Criticism

Does the doctrine of transcendental faith that is at the basis of this theory of anonymous Christianity not bear too strongly the marks of an elitist idealistic gnosiology? The great mass of people are saved by virtue of their *fides implicita* and their attitude of *bona fides*. The real relationships are known to the few who possess the "high gift of the wise." Rahner, whose entire theological disposition makes him turn away from an elitist attitude perhaps more than any other theologian, has himself raised this objection. His reference, however, to the marks of elitism in "sublime, aesthetic, logical, ethical and other forms of knowledge" which he believes apply to all men, but are only known to a few, is not convincing (at least for me). Full and explicit (!) knowledge of faith is, after all, a practical knowledge. In its distinctive character, it is incommensurable with purely scientific or idealistic forms of knowledge. It is possible to speak of an arcane knowledge in the case of a full knowledge of faith, but this *arcanum* cannot be the *arcanum* of a philosophical gnosis — an elitist idealism; it must be the *arcanum* of a practical knowledge. It cannot be the *arcanum* of a Socrates but must be the *arcanum* of Jesus, in other words, the practical arcane knowledge of the imitation of Christ.

Do we not have, in this form of transcendental Christianity, a form of overjustification and overidentification of Christianity in the face of the growing historical threat to its identity? Is the historical identity of Christian faith not fixed, in this theory, to a basic anthropological structure, according to which man is "always already," whether he wants to be or not, "with God"? It would certainly be a fundamental misunderstanding of Rahner's transcendental theology if we were to assume that its aim was simply to introduce Christian faith subsequently into a previously existing anthropological structure. The transcendental process works in the opposite direction, according to Rahner's explicit description of it. The actual historical experience of man in Christian faith is generalized and becomes the "categorical" precondition for our understanding of man as an absolutely transcendent being. The question remains, however, as to whether it is possible to generalize by means of speculative thought a historical experience (such as that of Christian faith), which is always threatened because of its historical character and whose identity is always endangered for the same reason. It may, in fact, only be possible to generalize this experience by means of a praxis for which no theological compensation can be found by transcendental reflection, but which must be remembered and narrated.

If we are to elaborate the idea of a narrative and practical Christianity further, we have first to extend our criticism, both that of Rahner's transcendental and idealistic theory and also (at least in outline) that of the universal-historical and idealistic conceptions. My criticism, then, is principally directed against the attempt to explain the historical identity of Christianity by means of speculative thought (idealism), without regard to the constitutive function of Christian praxis, the cognitive equivalent of which is narrative and memory.

A Fairy Story—to Read "Against the Grain"

To clarify what I mean by this criticism, I should like to recall one of the best known German fairy stories, that of the hare and the hedgehog. One Sunday morning, a hedgehog is going for a walk in a ploughed field and a hare teases him about his bandy legs. The hedgehog challenges the hare to a race in the furrows of the field. First, however, he goes home to breakfast because, as he tells the hare, he cannot run on an empty stomach. He then returns with his wife, who is exactly the same in appearance as her husband, and gets her to stand at the far end of the furrow. He himself stands at the other end beside the hare in another furrow. The hare falls for this trick. He runs and runs in his furrow, but the hedgehog is (in both positions) "always already" there. In the end, the hare falls dead from exhaustion on the field.

The "little ones" of this world, who are always slow and therefore deprived in life and for whose encouragement this fairy story was presumably written, may let me perhaps tell this story "against the grain," in other words, against its own fully justified intention and for a moment take the side of the hare, who runs and runs and in the end falls dead in the race, while the hedgehog wins by a cunning trick and does not even have to run. If we opt for the hare, we opt to enter the field of history, a field that can be measured in running the course of the race, in competition or in flight (one is reminded here of the images used in Pauline traditions for the historical and eschatological life of Christians). And this option for the hare also means that we must try to expose critically the idealistic guarantee of the threatened identity of Christianity. This guarantee leaves out of account the power of praxis to save the historical identity of Christianity and acts as a kind of theological hedgehog trick which aims to safeguard the identity and triumph of Christianity without the experience of the race (that is, without the experience of being threatened and possibly of being defeated).

The Exposure of the Hedgehog Trick, or a Criticism of the Transcendental and Idealistic Versions of the Guarantee of Identity

There are two versions of this hedgehog trick, both of which can be used to explain both the universal-historical and the transcendental attempt to undermine history.

The *first version* of the hedgehog trick stands for the universal-historical and idealistic approaches. Like the two hedgehogs, those who suggest these approaches have the course of history in view. Because they view it from both ends, however, there is no need to enter it. The hare runs and the hedgehog stands in a deceptive duplication at the control points of history as a whole. In this way, history is made into a movement of the so-called objective spirit which we have already seen through. And theology is made into a kind of information service for world history, but one that is consulted less and less by the public.

The ultimately promised saving meaning of history is not disclosed, as it were, while the course of that history is being run. It is not evoked, remembered, and narrated (for all men) as a practical experience of meaning in the middle of our historical life. It is, so to speak, rigidified into a definition for reflection that cannot be affected by collective historical fears or threats of catastrophe and is therefore not in need of any hope provided with expectation. The present state of meaning has had all its wrinkles ironed out and is free of all contradictions. It is, as it were, "hopelessly" total. There is only a very weak eschatological and apocalyptical sense of danger and of the needs of the age. This eschatological consciousness has been successfully removed from the theologies of history and transferred to the realm of individual history.

The *second version* of the hedgehog trick stands for the transcendental and idealistic approach, the idea of transcendental Christianity. The hare runs and the two hedgehogs are "always already" there. In the North German fairy story, the hedgehog husband and wife alternate with each other, calling, "I am here." By means of their transcendental omnipresence, they harass the hare to death. Is not — in this second version — the threatened historical identity of Christianity guaranteed for a too high price: the price of confusing identity with tautology? The two hedgehogs — the hedgehog's wife is exactly the same in appearance as her husband — stand for this tautology and the running hare stands for the possibility at least of historical identity. The running itself, during which it is also possible to fall flat on your face, belongs, together with its danger, to the guarantee of identity. Nothing can compensate for it transcendentally. In my opinion, everything else leads in the end to tautology — one hedgehog is exactly the same as the other, the beginning is like the end, paradise is like the end of time, creation is like the fulfillment and at the end the beginning repeats itself. History itself — with its forms of identity that are constantly threatened and in danger of being overcome — cannot intervene. The transcendental magic circle is complete and, like the two hedgehogs, it cannot be overcome *vae insuperabilibus*. One therefore suspects that the process of transcendentalization of the Christian subject may have been guided by a tendency to unburden and immunize. Would this process of transcendentalization not give Christianity a kind of omnipresence which would ultimately remove it from every radical threat in the sphere of history? Is the vanguard of the historical and apocalyptical attack made by Christianity and its identity not destroyed by this process of transcendentalization of the Christian subject, and is the battle therefore not prematurely broken off?

A New "But"

Can there be another point of departure for Christian theology apart from the one that insists that the universal meaning of history and the historical identity of Christianity is already established? How could universally historical meaning continue to be called into question for theology? Has history not been saved a long time ago in the definitive eschatological action of God in Jesus Christ? Is it not essential for theology to argue as both the approaches that are criticized here do, that is, transcendentally or universal-historically? Is Christian theology in this sense not necessarily idealistic? And should it therefore, for its own sake, not accept the criticism that it does not take history seriously with all its contradictions, antagonisms, struggles, and sufferings, and that it makes an "as if" problem of it? Does not every other attempt lead to a contradictory idea of a conditioned salvation or to a confusion of salvation and utopia?

But how can these idealistic "solutions" themselves avoid the danger of regarding the history of salvation as a totality without reference to the subject, in other words, of looking over the heads of the people who are bowed down under their own histories of suffering? Does this one,

universal history of salvation that is founded in Christ not take place in
the concrete mystical-political histories of salvation?

But how does this take place? And how is it possible to speak about it
if, in the case of salvation history, the very notion of history constituted
by concrete subjects is overlooked? Finally, should the salvation of the
whole of history that has been promised at the end of time be reduced
to a harmless teleological history of meaning in which it is no longer
possible to consider seriously, let alone provide a conscious theological
assessment of, the catastrophic element that is present in that history?

A Plea for a Narrative and Practical Christianity

It is because of the existence of these questions that I make a plea for
a narrative and practical structure of Christianity, its historical identity,
and its idea of eschatological salvation.

In this context, it is important to point to one very decisive factor.
As distinct from pure discourse or argument, narrative makes it possible
to discuss the whole of history and the universal meaning of history in
such a way that the idea of this universal meaning is not transferred to
a logical compulsion of totality or a kind of transcendental necessity. As
a result of this, the mystical-political histories of individuals would be of
secondary importance in comparison with the saving meaning of history
as a whole and could only be incorporated subsequently into the framework of a definitive history dissociated from the subjects. In the narrative
conception of Christian salvation, however, history and histories — the
one history of salvation and the many particular histories of salvation —
merge together without diminishing each other. The individual histories
do not take place without regard to the previously narrated history of
salvation and the history of salvation is able to assimilate the individual
histories. The narrated (and remembered) universality and definitiveness
of the meaning of history mean that the historical praxis of opposition
to meaninglessness and to the absence of salvation is not superfluous,
as though it were transcendentally or universal-historically guaranteed,
but indispensable.

The universality of the offer of salvation in Christianity does not have
the character of a transcendental or universally historical concept of universality. It has rather the character of an "invitation." The inviting *logos*
of Christianity does not in any sense compel. It has a narrative structure
with a practical and liberating intention. If this is expressed in Christological terms, it means that the salvation that is founded "for all men"
in Christ does not become universal via an idea, but via the intelligible
power of a praxis, the praxis of following Christ. This intelligibility of

Christianity cannot be transmitted theologically in a purely speculative way. It can only be transmitted in narrative — as a narrative and practical Christianity. It is also clear from this that the so-called historical crisis of identity of Christianity is not a crisis of the contents of faith, but rather a crisis of the Christian subjects and institutions which deny themselves the practical meaning of those contents, the imitation of Christ.

The imitation of Christ is a question of decisive importance for the version of the identity crisis that is served up every day in many varieties of the criticism of religion and ideology and which has become popular, within Christianity, in the catchphrase: "Yes to Jesus, no to the Church." What we have here is a deep suspicion, rooted in the prerational Christian consciousness, that the living identity of the Christian body with Jesus has become lost in later Christianity, that Christianity cast off its conformity to Christ a long time ago and that many of Jesus' intentions were long ago successfully taken over by other historical movements. This suspicion cannot be reduced simply by interpreting more subtly the historical attitude of Christianity, in other words, by a more scholarly form of hermeneutics and a more critical reconstruction of the history of Christianity. It can only be diminished by providing evidence of the spirit and power of Christianity in consistent imitation of Christ, in other words, by practical conformity to Christ. Our memories of the failure of Christianity and the deeply rooted disappointments felt by individuals and whole groups and classes of people cannot be theoretically explained away. For even successful historical research cannot exempt us from these collective memories of suffering, that is, we would not be regarded as in any sense justified in the presence of those memories. It is clear, then, that this version of our Christian identity crisis also compels us to accept the praxis of following Christ and points at the same time to the urgent need for a narrative and practical Christianity.

Conclusions

This narrative and practical Christianity of the following of Christ is a political Christianity, for the following of Christ always has a dual mystical and political structure. This mystical and political Christianity implies a criticism of that dominant form of Christianity which is making a last attempt to achieve universality by transforming the messianic religion of the following of Christ into a middle-class religion which functions as a legitimating ideology for the priorities, aspirations and security of middle-class society.

The *theology* of this narrative and practical Christianity makes necessary new *loci* and new subjects of theology. Alongside academic theology, which reflects the division of labor of middle-class societies, a new type of theology is called for which could perhaps be described as a mystical-political biography, that is, a theology which is fully aware of the historical and social situation of its subjects.

On the occasion of Karl Rahner's seventy-fifth birthday, I have tried to show that his theology can be understood as a biography in which the narrative elements form the substructure of the transcendental reflection. In this sense Rahner truly belongs to the classics: we can often find support for objections to his theories in the broader context of his own thinking.

Chapter 10

Theology in the New Paradigm

Political Theology

Paradigm Change in Theology?

Let me (incautiously) assume for the moment that there is something like "progress" in theology. How can this progress be assessed? Perhaps on the basis of paradigm change, in analogy to Kuhn's suggestion? I would hesitate here, and should like to put a number of questions, without aiming at completeness, and without claiming any competence in scientific theory.

What Kuhn understands by progress derives explicitly from an aetiological evolution logic,[1] and is therefore also formulated in neo-Darwinian terms.[2] But is the *logos* of Christian theology, with its underlying apocalyptic-eschatological structure, not molded by a different logic of time, history, and development (if indeed we can speak of development here at all)?[3] At all events, for the *logos* of this theology, "tradition" and "remembrance," for example, cannot simply be replaced by "historical reconstruction" on an evolutionistic basis. It is not evident how the evolutionary model could permit a normative use of history, let alone a "canonical" one.[4]

Is there such a thing as a "pure" history of theology at all, analogous to the "pure" history of science and to Kuhn's hermetic scientific community — a history of theology separate from church history, for example, or from political history? Is a new paradigm ever produced internally by theology at all? Is there any such thing as a theological paradigm change

---

1. In which — to take up a saying of the "Darwinian" Nietzsche — evolution aims at nothing except — evolution.
2. Cf. Thomas S. Kuhn, *The Structure of Scientific Revolutions* (Chicago, 1962), chap. 13. But see also Toulmin's criticism of Lakatos (Popper) taken up by Lamb in his "The Dialectic of Theory and Praxis in Paradigm Analysis," in *Paradigm Change in Theology: A Symposium for the Future*, ed. Hans Küng and David Tracy, trans. Margaret Köhl (New York: Crossroad, 1989), 63–109. Here the question about time and history could be reconsidered.
3. On the question about the relation between history and evolution, cf. J. B. Metz, *Faith in History and Society*, trans. D. Smith (London, 1980), chap. 10.
4. Cf. here ibid., chaps. 11 and 12.

123

independent of reformative processes in the context of the church? Is the history of theological thought not always shaped by the social history of religion and the church?

Who is the conscious subject of theology? What is the place where theology is done? Is this as unequivocally clear for theology as it is when we apply the paradigm theory to scientific history? Does not a change in the subjects of theology and the places where theology is practiced perhaps actually belong to the specific theological paradigm change?[5] Finally, are there not always several competing paradigms in theology — constitutionally, and not merely temporarily?[6]

I shall therefore use "paradigm" and "paradigm change" in theology in a rather broad sense.[7] As *criteria* for a "new paradigm in theology" I should like tentatively to propose the following: (a) the awareness of crisis and the capacity for dealing with it; and (b) the capacity for reduction. I mean this in two ways: first, as a nonregressive reduction of overcomplexity and wordiness — language-run-riot (in which the crises of theology are pushed below the surface and covered up);[8] and second, as the nontrivial reduction of doctrine to life, of doxography to biography, because the *logos* of theology always aims at a form of knowledge that is a *form of living*.[9] For the idea of God to which Christian theology is bound is in itself a practical idea. It continually cuts across the concerns of people who try "merely to think" it. The histories of new beginnings,

---

5. Cf. J. B. Metz, *A New Paradigm of Doing Theology?* (Lima, 1983). Cf. also *Doing Theology in New Places*, ed. J. B. Metz and J.-P. Jossua, *Concilium* (May 1978).

6. In the light of its content (cf. n. 9 below) and in the light of its subjects and the places where it is pursued (the theology of the religious orders, university theology, basis theology, and so on).

7. Modifications can also be found in contributions by Küng, Tracy, and Lamb in *Paradigm Change in Theology*, ed. Küng and Tracy

8. "Reduction" as the criterion of a theological paradigm change must not be confused semantically with the same term as it is employed in system theory.

9. Cf. here my attempt to interpret Karl Rahner's theology as a kind of new paradigm: "Karl Rahner – ein theologisches Leben," in J. B. Metz, *Unterbrechungen* (Gütersloh, 1981). I should also like in this connection to point to a paradigm discussion in modern Protestant theology which has meanwhile become a classic: the correspondence between Karl Barth and Adolf von Harnack, which was published sixty years ago. Barth stresses over against Harnack the apocalyptically tense crisis structure of faith, and the proclamation character of theology:

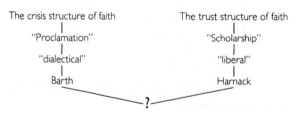

conversion, resistance, and suffering belong to the very definition of this idea of God. The pure concept "God" is the contraction, the shorthand, so to speak, of histories, in response to which theology must repeatedly decode its terms.[10]

I should like therefore to name the crises which provide the impulse for a paradigm change in theology, and shall then try to show why, and in what sense, the "new" theology which is able to absorb these crises productively and tries to achieve the reductions I have described, is a political theology, or has a political dimension.

The Crises

Let me mention three crises which have sparked off new ways of doing theology.[11] They are incidentally so constituted that their productive theological absorption is necessarily *ecumenical* in its very approach, not merely in its result.

1. *Theology in the face of the modern era:* that is, theology after the end of the religious and metaphysical views of the world — views that still provided the context for Reformation theology.

2. *Theology in the face of Auschwitz:* that is, theology after the end of idealism, or all systems of meaning without conscious subjects.

3. *Theology in the face of a socially divided and culturally polycentric worldwide church:* that is, theology at the end of its cultural monocentricism. In my view this "end" shelters within itself promising signs of a change.

The Political Dimension of Theology in the New Paradigm

The "new" theology which perceives these crises as fundamental crises of theology and which tries to overcome them in productive reduction is a "political" theology.

---

10. In this approach the difference between *logos* and myth, history and histories remains *within* theology.

11. On the following signs of crisis or of the End-time cf., among others, J. Habermas, *Legitimation Crisis*, trans. T. McCarthy (London, 1976); R. Spaemann, "Die christliche Religion und das Ende des modernen Bewusstseins," *Communio* 8 (1979): 251–70; J. B. Metz, *The Emergent Church*, trans. P. Mann (New York, 1981); L. Gilkey, "The New Watershed in Theology," *Soundings* (1981): 111–71.

Theology after the End of the Religious and Metaphysical Views of the World

The theological discernment and absorption of this end — that is, the productive grappling with the processes of the Enlightenment — bring to the fore the political dimension of theology under two aspects. Both these aspects have given rise to misunderstanding and semantic confusion in the past, and still do so today. This is because, on the one hand, people have tried to fit this political theology into the already existing divisions of theological labor. This has led to a misreading of its character as *fundamental theology* (see below). On the other hand, another misunderstanding was due to the fact that, after the Enlightenment, this political theology was identified with the legitimizing political theology of the pre-Enlightenment era. Its *critical* character was therefore overlooked.

a. With regard to the first point, the very project of a fundamental theology after the Enlightenment may be termed *political theology*. The disintegration of the religious and metaphysical world pictures has put an end to the era of theology's cognitive innocence. Theology must now come to terms with the denials of historical innocence through historicism, and with the denials of its social innocence through ideological criticism in both its bourgeois and its Marxist versions. Theology can no longer push the questions invoked here away from its center into the fringe zones of apologetics. Its very *logos* is affected.[12]

As fundamental theology, it can therefore no longer be content with the usual assignment of historical and social themes in theology to different divisions of labor. As fundamental theology it must be hermeneutics, and its hermeneutics must be political hermeneutics. For it cannot simply leave "history" to a separate historical theology, as if theology had any foundation without history and without a thinking subject.[13] Nor can it view "society" as the exclusive domain of social ethics, or the social teachings of the church,[14] as if theology's search for truth and witness to that truth had any foundation completely removed from social concerns and conflicts. Moreover, since the Enlightenment, a fundamental theology can no longer simply assume that the relation between theory

---

12. For the project of a practical fundamental theology as practical theology see Metz, *Faith in History and Society*, chaps. 1–7.

13. Cf. Tracy's chapter on hermeneutics, "Hermeneutical Reflections in the New Paradigm," in *Paradigm Change in Theology*, ed. Küng and Tracy. Recent discussions about the narrative structure of theology also belong here.

14. For criticism of this division of labor see now above all W. Kroh, *Kirche im gesellschaftlichen Widerspruch* (Munich, 1982). Here Kroh carries on the first detailed discussion between the new political theology and the traditions of Catholic social teaching.

and practice is, as far as it is concerned, sufficiently settled by way of the customary division of labor between systematic and practical theology. For to assume this would be to conceal from itself the practical foundation of all theological wisdom and the specific form, or Gestalt, its theory takes. Fundamental theology, that is to say, must be practical, political hermeneutics.[15] In my view, a fundamental theology of this kind must ultimately again take up the question about the cognitive subjects of theology, and the places where theology is to be done — a question which was supposed to have been dealt with by way of the division of labor in the church.[16]

b. Now, of course, the disintegration of religious and metaphysical world pictures in the Enlightenment must not be interpreted as if the result were an utterly demythologized and secularized world, with a total divorce between religion and politics.[17] Religion was not completely privatized, and politics was not entirely secularized.[18] Even politically "enlightened" societies have their political religions, with the help of which they seek to legitimize and stabilize themselves. We are familiar with this political religion in the "civil religion" of the United States, for example, as well as in what we in Germany call *bürgerliche Religion*. Although linguistically the two phrases mean the same thing (for example, *bürgerliches Recht* = civil law), civil religion and *bürgerliche Religion* can by no means simply be equated, for they derive from very different political cultures.[19] So when in Germany neoconservatism also recommends the introduction of a "civil religion,"[20] this amounts ultimately to a reproduction of the traditional patterns in which politics is legitimized by religion — in the guise of political theology in its classic form.[21] Of

---

15. H. Peukert, *Science, Action, and Fundamental Theology* (Engl. trans., Cambridge, Mass., 1984), has developed this approach and carried it further in discussion with contemporary theories of science and action. Cf. also Lamb's paper and the work of his own he cites there. From the point of view of liberation theology, of particular importance is the epistemological work by C. Boff and F. Castillo, *Theologie aus der Praxis des Volkes* (Munich, 1978). Boff includes criticism of J. B. Metz, J. Moltmann, and D. Sölle.

16. Cf. n. 5.

17. "The dialectic of Enlightenment" has already taught us how much the notion of the total demythologization or secularization of the world, and the concept of progress molded by this idea, became the real myth of early modern times.

18. For important observations here and on the definition of the tasks of a new political theology see F. Fiorenza, "Religion und Politik," in *Christlicher Glaube in moderner Gesellschaft* 27 (Freiburg, 1982).

19. Cf. J. Habermas, "Neokonservative Kulturkritik in den USA und in der Bundesrepublik," *Merkur* (November 1982).

20. Recently, above all H. Lübbe, following N. Luhmann.

21. Cf. here the critical comments by J. Moltmann, "Das Gespenst einer Zivilreligion," *Evangelische Kommentare* (March 1983). I should like to associate myself specifically with his criticism.

course both political religions, American and German, serve to politicize religion — a politicization which means that religion is assigned a strict social purpose: it is functionalized.

But it is just this politicization of religion which political theology criticizes, and for two reasons. On the one hand, it criticizes it as religion, since political theology contests a religion which acts as legitimation myth and which purchases its discharge from society's criticism of religion through the suspension of its claim to truth. On the other hand, it criticizes the politicization of religion on theological grounds, contesting all theologies which, appealing to their nonpolitical character, become preeminently theologies of just this political religion. If we do not want to establish the essence of religion in politics, not even an enlightened politics, we must not suppress theology's political dimension.

Of course this interpretation also provokes questions, and above all this one: if neither civil religion nor its German equivalent is available as the place where, since the Enlightenment, religion and politics can legitimately be reconciled theologically, what then? How then can the universal norms of Christianity be brought into harmony with political life at all, since that political life certainly cannot and must not revert to the time before the achievements of the political Enlightenment — the separation of powers, the right to opposition, liberty of opinion, and so forth? Do these universal norms make themselves felt when questions about ultimate goals crop up in political life, not merely questions about methods and their application? That is to say, do these norms make their impact when prevailing conditions themselves come under pressure and require legitimation — when a political ethic is required, not merely as an ethic for order but as *an ethic for change* ?[22]

Auschwitz — or Theology after the End of Idealism

Here Auschwitz stands for the end of the modern era. In this context we have to notice first of all that the catastrophe of Auschwitz takes on paradigmatic character through its very incomparability. It points theology's historical and political conscience away from the singular "history" to the plural "histories of suffering," which cannot be idealistically explained, but can only be recollected in the context of a practical intent.[23] But which theology does not live from a catastrophic background, either

22. See here as long ago as 1969, J. B. Metz in *Diskussion zur "politischen Theologie,"* ed. H. Peukert (Munich, 1969). At present this question, for example, is discussed under the heading of "monotheism and politics."
23. Cf. J. B. Metz, *Faith in History and Society*, chap. 9.

by turning its back on it — that is, idealistically — or by being profoundly chafed and disturbed by it?

There is no meaning which one could salvage by turning one's back on Auschwitz, and no truth which one could thereby defend. Theology therefore has to make an about-face, a turn which will bring us face to face with the suffering and the victims. And this theology is political theology. Its hermeneutics is a political hermeneutics, a hermeneutics in the awareness of danger.[24] It criticizes the high degree of apathy in theological idealism, and its defective sensibility for the interruptive character of historical and political catastrophes.

This political theology after Auschwitz is not a theology in terms of a system. It is theology in terms of human subjects, with a practical foundation. It continually introduces into public awareness "the struggle for recollection," for the recollecting knowledge which is related to the human subjects concerned. For this theology, the "system" can no longer be the place of theological truth — not, at least, since the catastrophe of Auschwitz, which no one can ignore without cynicism or can allow to evanesce into an "objective" system of meaning.

This theology formulates the question about God in its oldest and most controversial form, as the theodicy question — though not in an existentialist version but in a political one. It begins with the question about the deliverance of those who have suffered unjustly, the victims of our history and the defeated. It continually brings this question anew into political awareness as indictment, and expounds the concept of a strict universal solidarity, which also includes the dead, as a practical and political idea, on which the fate of human beings as clear and evident subjects depends.

For without this solidarity the life of human beings as subjects tends more and more toward anthropomorphism. The public invitation to apply for the post as successor to the human being as subject has already gone out. The applicant is to have no recollection of past suffering and is to be tormented by no catastrophes. *Time* magazine has already portrayed the successful candidate on its front cover, as the man of the year for 1983: the robot, an intelligence without memory, without feeling and without morals.[25]

---

24. Important elements for a "hermeneutics in the face of danger" may be found in W. Benjamin's work; cf. O. John's pertinent dissertation, " ... *und dieser Feind hat zu siegen nicht aufgehört." Die Bedeutung Walter Benjamins für eine Theologie nach Auschwitz* (Münster, 1983).

25. Cf. here in connection with the work of Metz and Peukert, M. Lamb, *Solidarity with Victims* (New York, 1982).

Theology at the End of Its Cultural Monocentricism

Is our paradigm discussion not too Eurocentrically aligned from the outset? I must ask this, because it is only in the light of this question that I
can discuss the political dimension of the "new" theology adequately. It
is a fact that the church no longer merely has a Third World church but
is a Third World church with, historically, West European origins. What
does this fact mean for Catholic theology, for example?

On the one hand it means that the social antagonism in the world is
moving to the center of attention in the church and in theology. Conditions which are directly inconsistent with the gospel, such as exploitation
and oppression or racism, are becoming challenges to theology. They demand that faith be formulated in categories of resistance and change.
Thus theology is impelled to become political by its own *logos*.

On the other hand, in this new situation in which the Church finds
itself, a process of theological significance is emerging which we should
not fail to take into account in our discussion about a paradigm change.
The Church is on the move from a culturally more or less monocentric
European and North American Church to one that is worldwide and
culturally polycentric. In order at least to indicate the theological import
of this transition, I should like[26] hypothetically to divide the history of
theology and the church, up to the present day, into three eras: a first,
relatively brief, founding era of Jewish Christianity; a second, very long
era, in a more or less homogeneous cultural area — the age of the gentile
Christianity that grew up on Hellenistic soil, the West European culture
and civilization that was bound up with that and which lasted down
to our own day; and a third era, the era of a worldwide cultural polycentricism in the Church and theology, which is emerging at the present
time. In this era the modern division between the churches, for example,
appears mainly as an internal fate affecting European Christendom.[27]

Of course, the end of cultural monocentricism does not mean disintegration into an arbitrary or random contextual pluralism. Nor does it
mean the enthronement of a new, non-European monocentricism in the
Church and in theology. The Church's original Western history, which in
concrete terms was always also a history of guilt where non-European

---

26. Following a suggestion of Karl Rahner's about the beginnings of a genuinely worldwide church in Vatican II; cf. his "Concern for the Church," *Theological Investigations* 20
(London, 1981).

27. Of course, in this hypothesis I have to assume much which I cannot discuss and sub-
stantiate here; for example, that there really is such a thing as this mutual polycentricism,
and that it has not already been corrupted in germ by the profane Europeanization of the
world which we call technology or technological civilization — that is, through the worldwide rule of Western rationality, in which far more of the politics, history, and anthropology
of Europe is concealed than the technocrats of all political colors would have us believe.

cultures were concerned, will remain an immanent part of the cultural polycentrism of the Church and theology. But what is at stake now is mutual inspiration and mutual productive assimilation. This seems to me to be important for our European outlook on the churches and theology of the Third World. For I see a reforming impulse coming upon Western Christianity from there and, linked with that, the offer of a "paradigm change" in theology as well. I can do no more than indicate that here, in the context of the political dimension of theology which I have been asked to talk about.[28]

With us this new beginning is associated rather abstractly with concepts such as base communities, liberation theology, and so forth. But here the gospel is related in a highly direct and immediate way to the specific political conditions in which people live. This "application" generally seems to us too naive, too premodern, too simplistic, in view of our own overcomplex situation, which has been heightened into extreme abstraction, particularly in the context of all the problems of interpretation in scripture and tradition which have accumulated in our theology ever since the Enlightenment, and which may be summed up under the catchword of "hermeneutics." But if we examine the matter more closely, it becomes evident that in this "application" we see a new form of theological hermeneutics, which I should like to call a political hermeneutics of danger. The awareness of danger as a basic category of a theological hermeneutics has a sound biblical foundation. The flash of danger lights up the whole biblical landscape; danger, present and impending, runs through all the biblical utterances, especially in the New Testament. As we know, the discipleship narratives in the synoptic gospels are not simply entertaining stories. They are not really even didactic stories. They are stories told in the face of danger: they are dangerous stories. And we have only to read John (15:18–19, for instance) or Paul (for example 2 Cor. 4:8–1): what do we understand about texts like these and their *logos* if, and as long as, the awareness of danger is systematically screened out in our hermeneutics?

Now, this political hermeneutics of danger is certainly reductive — to some degree oversimplifying — and that in the sense of the reductions I named at the beginning as criteria for a paradigm change: practice returns home to pure theory, logic is joined again by mysticism, resistance and suffering once more find their proper place in the theological definition of grace and Spirit. If then there really is "progress" in theology,

---

28. More detail may be found in my "Aufbruch zur Reformation," *Süddeutsche Zeitung* (April 9–10, 1983). Cf. also Metz, "Toward the Second Reformation," in *The Emergent Church.*

and anything like a paradigm change, should we not have to pay particular attention to new impulses like these in the culturally polycentric space for learning offered by the world church and the worldwide Christian faith?[29] Are these things not always bound up with the reformative situations in which Christianity "returns to its roots"?[30]

---

29. Of course, this raises the question how Christian universalism can be so understood in the encounter with other religions and cultures that it does not simply, without more ado, "imperialistically" integrate and subordinate them, but discerns them in their authentic message. I have tried to offer a solution in my reflections on the narrative-practical understanding of Christianity (as distinct from a transcendental-idealistic one) in *Faith in History and Society*, chap. 9. It seems to me that this approach also offers an indication of how the deadlocks of a Christian absolutism in the encounter with other religions and cultures could be solved.

30. Could we not, therefore, after all tentatively include the new paradigm of theology under the heading of "liberation"? If, for the moment, we start from the assumption that the paradigm that has hitherto molded modern theology was "liberty," then the paradigm change in theology would be the change from liberty to liberation. Cf. here my reflections in "Toward the Second Reformation" in *The Emergent Church*, and the references in n. 28 above. In *The Emergent Church*, in the same chapter, I also discuss the dilemma of Catholic theology in the face of the "liberty" paradigm.

Part 3

Hoping Against Hope

Chapter 11

Communicating
a Dangerous Memory

Introduction

I will not deny that I am very much honored to have the chance to talk to you today. You heard something *about* me yesterday; now you will hear something *from* me, and I hope that you'll not be too disappointed. Before I left this morning, some of my colleagues at St. Mary's Hall asked me whether I wouldn't prefer to go to the football game today. I said no, but if it had been soccer...!

Communicating a dangerous memory — there may be two possible approaches to this topic: one, more systematic, and another one more autobiographical. So, as you know, we agreed with one another — Fred Lawrence and Matt Lamb and I, and Sebastian Moore, too, I think — that we'll do it autobiographically. But let me just mention a systematic approach to this question, communicating a dangerous memory. You probably know that "dangerous memory" is one of the basic categories of the new political theology, at least as far as I have developed it during the last eighteen or twenty years. So whenever I am explaining the background and position of political theology in today's theology, I am talking about at least three competing paradigms within today's Catholic theology. And Fred has already mentioned these paradigms: the neo-Scholastic one, which still prevails much more than we should accept; the so-called idealist or transcendental paradigm, very powerfully developed by my great teacher and friend, Karl Rahner; and another paradigm, which I call a postidealist or political paradigm of doing theology, that includes this new type of political theology as well as most of liberation theology.

Whenever a new paradigm arises, this is due to certain criteria, and the most important criterion for a paradigm-shift within theology, at least as I understand it, is perceiving and dealing with new crises stemming from the historical and socially rooted character of theology. This type of political theology understands today's theology as being faced with three crises or three challenges, three "end phenomena." The first is the Marx-

ist challenge, or theology faced with the end of its cognitive innocence
and with the end of a dualistic understanding of history. The second is
the Auschwitz challenge: theology faced with the end of idealism or of
all systems of meaning which can prescind from historically identifiable
subjects. And the third crisis is the Third World challenge: the challenge
of the socially antagonistic and culturally polycentric world; that is, theology faced with the end of its so-called Eurocentricity. Political theology
tries to deal with these crises, to face up to these challenges.

But I do not want to talk about political theology and dangerous memory in political theology in the perspective of this systematic approach.
I would prefer, as we agreed, an autobiographical approach, which is
not without systematic relevance. And this is true because, in spite of
many prejudices, it is precisely this political type of doing theology and
this political mysticism that at least taught me to say "I" in theology, to
cease orienting myself toward concepts of the system and start orienting myself toward concepts of the subject, and to see through Christian
theology's high content of apathy insofar as it is idealistic and without
an identifiable subject. Theology, precisely as a politically sensitive theology, takes on the traits of biography; but the orientation toward the
subject, toward the countenance, toward functioning-in-the-face-of, be-
stows on theology traits of narrative and memory. This does not make it
subjectivist or serve to stylize theological individuality, but heightens its
sensitivity to the concrete responsibility encountered in controversial talk
about God. And I think it is imperative to learn this theological saying,
"I," when confronting today's challenges, when confronting our history
in its negativities. So this is one of the systematic reasons for talking
biographically within theology.

The second reason is that I want to give an account of the dangerous
memory, which was and is a basic category of my theology, in the face
of my own experiences. And the third reason is that political theology
is nothing but *theology*. And theology which does not deceive itself and
others finally is nothing but theo-logy, that is, the attempt to talk about
God in the face of a great danger. Every authentic type of theology must
be political. That is one of the presuppositions of this way of doing theology. And thus "political theology" is a pleonastic or redundant phrase.
I hope that I can show you something of that now in this reflection.

My God Question

So I start with talking about my faith in God, or how I as theologian
understand this. The treatment of the God question always contains biographical elements, because relevant speech about God always examines

and calls into question our preconceived notions about life and existence, our interests, our memories, our experiences.) And this means that theology cannot ignore the field of one's personal experiences when speaking about God. At the center of *my* theological speech about God lies the theological-political treatment of the so-called theodicy problem — the question of God in the face of human suffering, which since the Enlightenment has been turned into a question of anthropodicy — the question of justifying human beings who are now subjects of the process of history in the face of the misery and suffering of other people. This modern form of anthropodicy is nothing but a coded form of theodicy, but we will not talk about that here. That the theodicy problem stands at the center of my doing theology is due to my personal experiences. And I would like to use two more or less biographical events as examples to show you how memory functions as "dangerous memory" not only within the great realm of theology in the world but within one's own life.

The first event occurred when I was 16 years old, at the end of the Second World War. I was taken out of school and pressed into military service. It was 1945. With barely any military training I was sent to the front, and at that time the Americans had already crossed the Rhine River. My whole company was made up of young soldiers of about the same age. One evening my company commander sent me back to the battalion headquarters with a message. Throughout the night I strayed through burning farms and villages. When I returned to my company the next morning, I found all my comrades dead. The company had been attacked by planes and tanks and was completely wiped out. I saw only the lifeless faces of my comrades, those same comrades with whom I had but days before shared my childhood fears and my youthful laughter. I remember nothing but a soundless cry. I strayed for hours alone in the forest. Over and over again, just this silent cry! And up until today I see myself so. (Behind this memory all my childhood dreams have vanished.)

Perhaps in this way I can make clear to you why the so-called theodicy problem stands at the center of my theological considerations. Perhaps in this way I can also make clear why the theodicy problem must be posed, as far as I understand it, as a question of the suffering of others and as the personally experienced past suffering of others. For me the theodicy question, the basic theological question — and theology is a culture of questions, not of answers — is not "Who saves me?" but rather, "Who saves you?" And all those who attend my lectures know that I begin not *the* with the question, "What happens to me when I suffer, when I die?" but *"other"* rather with, "What happens to you when you suffer, when you die?"

In order to show you that such a personal experience can also become a public consciousness within at least some regions of our church life and some communities, I would like to point to the following. A basic form of Christian hope is also determined by this memory. The question, "What dare I hope?," is transformed for me into the question, "What dare I hope for you and, in the end, also for me?" Fred has mentioned already the synod document, *Our Hope*, of the German bishops' conference of some years ago. I wrote the draft of that document, and if I may quote just a few phrases from it:

> Relying only on ourselves? How could that possibly end except in melancholy, barely concealed despair or blind, selfish optimism? To dare to hope in God's Kingdom always means entertaining this hope for others and therefore also for oneself. Only when our hope is inseparable from hope for others, in other words, only when it automatically assumes the form and motion of love and communion, does it cease to be petty and fearful, a hopeless reflection of our egotism. We for our part have crossed over from death to life; this we know, because we love our brothers.[1]

I have met in the face of communities of the Third World — but not only there — persons in whose suffering, in whose struggle, in whose sorrow, and in whose courage I can identify the symbols of the kingdom of God. And I can make this identification more easily through them than through my own life. Through my experience of these persons and these communities I can relate the pictures and parables about the kingdom of God finally also to myself. You see, this is my personal approach to this question, which I consider to be the basic question of today's theology, the so-called theodicy question.

But of course there is also another biographical event which has to be mentioned and was mentioned earlier in this conference. For me, the German theologian, there is an event which I should never forget. I call it the Auschwitz challenge. It is one of the indications that Christian theology is not a type of faceless metaphysics. It is rather an appeal to and a witness of truth in history: "The Word became flesh." Historical situations are inherent in the *logos* of theology. Somewhere and somehow I have become aware of the situation in which I try to do theology. It took much time, and this is due to the fact that my great teacher, Karl Rahner, to whom I owe the greatest debt and the best that I have ever learned in theology, never spoke in his theology about this catastrophe. So it took a long time for me to think of that, and to become aware of this situation in which I try to do theology and outside of which I have no

---

1. "Our Hope: A Confession of Faith for This Time," *Study Encounter* 12, nos. 1–2 (1976): 77.

idea how to get my theological bearings. And this is for me, the German theologian, "after Auschwitz." Auschwitz represents here the crisis of so-called modernity, but above all a crisis of my Christian theology.

At the outset, one must take into account that the catastrophe of Auschwitz, precisely because of its uniqueness, acquires a provocative character. This catastrophe cannot be integrated into *the* history which we usually talk about in our different types of modern theological hermeneutics: universal-history hermeneutics, for example, of my friends like Wolfhart Pannenberg, Jürgen Moltmann, and others. They talk about *the* history as such. The catastrophe of Auschwitz directs theology away from the singular of "history" to the plural of "histories of sufferings" which cannot be idealistically explained but rather can only be remembered with a practical intention. Because of the way Auschwitz was or was not present in theology, I slowly became aware of the high content of apathy in theological idealism and its inability to confront historical experience in spite of all its prolific talk about historicity. There was no theology in the whole world which talked so much about historicity as German theologies. Yet they only talked about historicity; they did not mention Auschwitz. Obviously there is no meaning of history one can save with one's back turned to Auschwitz; there is no truth of history which one can defend, and no God in history which one can worship, with one's back turned to Auschwitz. This was one of the starting points — not the only one, of course — of any theology as political theology: saying that theology must take seriously the negativity of history in its interruptive and catastrophic character (by which history is distinguished from nature and its anonymous evolutionary processes). The catastrophes must be remembered with a practical-political intention so that this historical experience does not turn to tragedy and thus bid the history of freedom farewell. That is a great seduction: to face these catastrophes and then end up with a kind of tragic consciousness. We are not allowed to do that. What I experienced was that we have a duty to face these catastrophes and remember them with a practical-political intention so that they might never be repeated. This shows that the political paradigm of theology is due neither to a foolish overactivity nor to the transparent attempt at duplicating the already existing political patterns. It is rather due to the struggle for history in its unfathomable histories of suffering, the struggle for history as the constitutionally threatened locus of theological truth-finding.

It is because we believe in a definite eschatological meaning of history that we can face the negativities, the catastrophes, without irrationally dividing or denying our responsibilities, without developing excuse mechanisms. It is for that reason that I am upset about the use of the term

holocaust, for example, in my country today. I have many friends within
the peace movement, but I criticize them for one thing, and that is the
semantic confusion of the use of such a word. Today the word *holocaust*
is very often mentioned in German newspapers, more or less every day,
but no one would think of Auschwitz when he hears the word *holocaust*.
They all think of the nuclear holocaust. And why do they do it? What I
tell them is that it is much easier to talk about the possible future catastrophe in which we are the victims, than to talk about a past catastrophe
in which we were the actors. But we will not overcome a catastrophe
like the one which we call the nuclear "collapse" or "holocaust" —
never use the word *holocaust* for that — if we forget the catastrophe
of our own history. That is teaching on the level of political theology,
as I understand it.

This political theology formulates the God question again in its oldest
and most controversial form, namely, as the theodicy question, though
naturally not in its existentialist but rather in its political version. It begins
with the question of those who suffer unjustly, of the victims and the
vanquished of our history. How can one ask, after Auschwitz, about one's
own salvation outside of this perspective? That is my question. Political
theology repeatedly injects this question into public consciousness and
elucidates it as a question on which the fate of humanity depends. The
memoria passionis, the memory of suffering, which is a radical biblical
category, becomes a universal category, a category of rescue. And if I may
indicate again how a personal theological experience can become a public
experience, a communicative experience within the church, I would like
to quote another passage from the synod document *Our Hope*. It says:

> But to forget or suppress this question...is to behave in a pro-
> foundly inhuman way. For it means forgetting and suppressing the
> sufferings of the past and accepting without protest the pointless-
> ness of this suffering. In the last resort, no happiness enjoyed by the
> children can make up for the pain suffered by the fathers, and no
> social progress can atone for the injustice done to the departed. If
> we persist too long in accepting the meaninglessness of death and
> in being indifferent to death, all we shall have left to offer even to
> the living will be banal promises. It is not only the growth of our
> economic resources which is limited, as we are often reminded to-
> day, but also the resources of meaning, and it is as if our reserves
> here are melting away and we are faced with the real danger that
> the impressive words we use to fuel our own history — words like
> freedom, liberation, justice, happiness — will in the end have all
> their meaning drained out of them.

Without this *memoria passionis*, the life of humans as subjects becomes increasingly an anthropomorphism. The public advertisement for a successor to the human subject, a successor who has no memory of past suffering and is no longer tortured by catastrophes, has already begun. *Time*, for example, has recently placed a picture of this successor on one of its covers: the robot, a smoothly functioning machine, an intelligence without remembrance, without pathos, and without morals. And thus, in the fight for history and historical consciousness, a new front has been opened for theology: the front of what I call the evolutionarily infected lassitude about history, the tending toward a so-called posthistoricity in our late modernity. To speak critically about this evolutionistic mentality does not mean to favor a fundamentalist position with regard to the question of creation and evolution. It is much more the background of the question, "What is the basic symbol for understanding today's scientific life?" And for me it is very, very powerful, not just for scientists, but for popular thinking: the quasi-religious symbol of what you might call — though it can be misunderstood — evolutionary mentality.

But now, very briefly, I have a second remark to add to this Auschwitz biography of my own. You should not forget that I come from a Bavarian village, a Catholic Bavarian village of about 10,000 people. I told you that at the end of the war I was about 16 years old; and just thirty miles away from this village, from this little town, there was a concentration camp. And in this concentration camp Dietrich Bonhoeffer was murdered. We never talked about this. As a young child I never heard about it. You see, my father was already dead and my mother was afraid and a pious woman. Later on, when I talked to her about that event, she always denied having known anything about it, though she — well, it was a kind of suppressed knowing. That is why I am talking about this subject. After becoming theologically aware of my post-Holocaust situation, I also asked myself what sort of faith it must have been that allowed us to go on believing undisturbed during the Nazi time. Was it not in the end only a purely believed-in faith, as I call it; a faith without compassion but with a belief in compassion which, under the mantle of believing it was compassionate, cultivated the apathy that allowed us Christians to go on believing with our backs turned to such a catastrophe? I call this type of believing *bürgerliche Religion*, bourgeois religion.) *middle class* Whatever may be the truth of the matter, the critical use of the concept "bourgeois religion" thus has a solidly theological and not primarily a sociological basis. That is what I want to point to.

Was it not a lack of politically sensitive spirituality which led us into our grievous error? If we had known more explicitly that we Christians are also responsible for emerging structures and processes, that we are not only responsible for what we do or omit, but what we do or omit in regard to others; if we had known that more clearly and explicitly, would we then not have resisted in time? Resisted in time. You see, when I criticize this period of my history, I do not say that they all should have been heroes, because resisting against the Nazi regime in 1940 was already heroic. It always meant death. But if we had been sensitive to the danger, if theology had had that hermeneutics of danger, we might have resisted in time. You see, resistance is a question of the schedule, not of heroism, and it can be an expression of grace to resist in time. We were graceless. How did we understand our Christianity? In specific distinction to other great religions of the world, as a Christian, one can be too pious and too mystical! The one and undivided discipleship of Jesus contains always a mystical *and* a situational-political element. They mirror one another, and that is specifically Christian. I quote again the passage, mentioned yesterday, from the document *Our Hope:*

> Jesus was neither a fool nor a rebel: but He could obviously be mistaken for either. In the end he was derided by Herod as a fool and handed over by his own countrymen as a rebel to be crucified. Anyone who follows him ... must allow for the same possibility of being the victim of such confusion.

(Theology must not unveil but respect the "incognito of Jesus"; it belongs to the saving history of the passion, and theology has to make clear that the present misery of our Christianity is not that we are considered as fools and rebels too often, but rather, practically never.) This theology can reclaim, as far as I see it, the traditions of this dangerous Jesus in the history of the religious orders, and it can refer today to the new mystical and political experiences of the emerging churches, the basic community churches within the poor churches of the earth, and can learn from them.

This kind of talk can imply a kind of aesthetic radicalism, at least for the German theology professor, doing theology under very privileged conditions of working and living, and being at the same time obliged to talk about the poor and homeless and obedient Jesus and the Christian task to follow him. You very often are in a dilemma, you see. Many of my colleagues give up talking about this question; they just talk about scientific questions — what they call scientific, though mostly disregarded by those who are authentic scientists. Or they may fall into the trap of what I call an aesthetic radicalism. In order to avoid that, I try to talk about those who really follow, to be close to them, and to participate with them. I started to talk about the subjective and the practical foundation of such a theology. That is what I meant when I began to talk about a statement which Matthew Lamb made yesterday about the church being an institution delivering a dangerous memory within the systems of our society, an institution of social-critical freedom.

The Dangerous Jesus

Let me finally talk about this category, the dangerous Jesus. Where is it from? Some colleagues of mine would say, "You're talking about apocalyptic." In one of the last conversations I had with Karl Rahner he said, "Well, try to do it, but don't forget that you can't just talk about it, you have to convince people." I was very critical of his distinction between eschatology and apocalyptic, which he introduced very powerfully into Catholic theology.

"Who is close to me is close to the fire; who is far from me is far from the Kingdom." This is the word of Jesus delivered to us, outside the canon, by Origen. It is dangerous to be close to Jesus; it is to be inflammable, to risk catching fire. Yet only in the face of the danger does there shine the vision of the Kingdom of God, which through him has come closer. "Danger" apparently is a basic category for the self-understanding of the "new life" in the New Testament. The lightning of danger illuminates the entire biblical landscape. Danger and peril are found everywhere in the New Testament. In the case of the synoptic gospels, the stories of discipleship are not entertaining stories and not educating ones. They are stories in the face of danger; in short, they are "dangerous stories." They invite us not to contemplate, but to follow, and only in the adventure of this following do they reveal their saving truth. When Jesus says, "Come and see," a German answer to that, a German proverb, is "Wo kamen wir hin wenn alle sagten, 'Wo kamen wir hin?', und keiner ginge und schaue wohin man käme wenn man ginge?" Oh, I can't translate it! "Where would we get to if everyone would say, 'Where would we get to?,' and no one would have a look at where we would get if we went," or something like that. The proverb points to this dangerous character of the invitation of Jesus, of these small stories, these stories about a homeless, suffering man from Nazareth, which have built our understanding of world history.

And in John we read: "Remember the word I said unto you: the servant is not greater than his lord. If they have persecuted me they will also persecute you." Or in Paul: "We are troubled on every side, but not distressed; we are perplexed but not in despair; persecuted but not forsaken; cast down but not destroyed." This dialectics of danger, this experience of danger — every one of you knows these passages from the liturgy, in what we call spirituality; but that is not due just to this division of labor, as if this is for spirituality and theology has nothing to do with it. We will not understand if we do not admit the category of danger into our theology. What do we know of the New Testament if in our understanding and interpreting the presence of danger is systematically disregarded in the name of enlightenment, in the name of demythologizing the New Testament, or whatever; if we erase the horizon of danger or paint over it — that horizon which holds together the whole New Testament panorama? What do we understand? I would say that one of the prophecies of the emerging church in the Third World and of liberation theology is that they understand that theology has to be done in the face of danger. Doing theology in the face of danger always implies a kind of simplification, a reduction: in the face of danger, mysticism returns to logic, praxis returns to theory, the experience of resistance and suffering returns into the experience of grace and spirit. These kinds of reductions are signs that Christianity is taking hold of its own roots. We in Germany also have a kind of reduction today. We talk about "short formulae of faith." That is the danger you now face. Because the core, the heart of Christianity cannot be concentrated in one dogma. It is between dogma and practice: that is Christianity; that is what the emerging churches understand, and that is why we have to learn from them.

What is behind our critique of the apocalyptic symbols? Is it the will toward enlightenment of the uncomprehended power of myth in these apocalyptic traditions, or is it perhaps the will to evade the dangerous Christ and so to contain the danger, or at least to push it aside into the practically extraterritorial realm of individual death? Most likely both of these are at work. For we are talking about apocalyptic questions only: when the individual incurs a crisis of identity in the face of suffering and death. But this means to make death more meaningless than it had ever been in the old tradition of Christianity, because the apocalyptic traditions of the end of the world were always combined and connected with questions: Who is the Lord of our time? To whom belong the processes of the world? Who is the subject of history? But they are practically forgotten in theology. We have to remember that there is not a history of the world on the one side and a history of salvation on the other side; what we call the history of salvation, as I understand it, is that history of the world in which you have an indestructible hope for past sufferings. That implies worshiping a power for which the past is still accessible: God.

Above all, we cannot forget this evading, evading the dangerous Christ, and it is not for want of trying, for the whole of history *anno Domino*, after Christ, may be interpreted as a maneuver to evade the dangerous Christ. In the context of this evasion there arises a Christianity — and I say this not in a denouncing manner but rather with a touch of sadness and helplessness — fashioned after a bourgeois homeland religion, *eine bürgerliche Heimatreligion*, rid of danger but also rid of consolation. For a Christianity which is not dangerous and which is unendangered also does not console. Or am I grossly mistaken? In some regions of Christianity I see emerging counterimages to such a placating bourgeois religion: for example, in those poor churches which understand their faithfulness to Christ also as liberation, and seek it as liberation in the face of danger. Is it presumptuous to accept that perhaps here, in these communities, a clearer concept breaks forth of what it means to be close to Jesus, close to him of whom it should be said, "Who is close to me is close to the fire"? *Christianity as Dangerous*

(The fatal disease of religion and of theology is not naiveté, but rather banality.) And theology can become banal whenever its commentary on life serves only to repeat that which without it — and often against it — has already become part of the common modern consensus. The naiveté of theology lies in ambush for these commonplaces. It does this, for example, by lingering with texts and images such as those in the apocalyptic traditions and by holding its own in the face of them at least a bit longer than the modern consensus and the anonymous pressure of modern civilization allow. At least a bit longer: that is naiveté — not a second naiveté, but naiveté. You cannot make a construction of language. That is a question of the reserves of meaning and the reserves of resistance in humankind; and if we had lost all naiveté, we would not have theologians telling us that there must be a second type or a second-order naiveté. No. Theology does not seek specifically to reconcile itself with its traditions by the use of thousands of subtle modifications, but rather to spell out its tradition as a dangerous subversive memory for the present. These thousands and thousands of modifications: are they not naiveté?

Just two brief examples in which this naiveté functions and of course can be heard, and you can laugh at it. Pointing to the apocalyptic symbol, religion wants to scandalize or (let me use the other term) to interrupt the dominant understanding of the human being in modernity, and to resist this understanding at least for a brief moment. It would be enough if we tried to do it for moments! It seeks to interrupt that understanding of the human being that is prevalent today within all blocs: the Faustian-Promethean human being. It seeks to interrupt that concept in which the coming human being is designed without the dark background of sorrow, suffering, guilt, and death. The rebellion of the apocalyptic symbols is turned against the human being empty of secrets, incapable of mourning and therefore incapable of being consoled; more and more unable to remember and so more easily manipulated than ever; more and more defenseless against the threatening apotheosis of banality and against the stretched-out death of boredom; a human being whose dreams of happiness finally are nothing but the dreams of an unhappiness free from suffering and longing. That is the front along which we are fighting when we recall the apocalyptic traditions.

Second, pointing to the apocalyptic symbols, theology wants to interrupt, to scandalize, the dominant understanding of time and history in modernity and to resist it at least for a moment. This resistance, this kind of interruption of our common consensus, is even more difficult to understand and practically cannot be freed from the suspicion of being deviant or being nonsense. I admit this because I am not sure about it; I tell you, because this is a communicative exchange here. No wonder that most theologians agree with the modern consensus, or that they see in these apocalyptic texts and symbols nothing but the projection of archaic fears. Whenever religion hands down, passes on, these texts and symbols and perceives in them elements of a dangerous memory, it does not do it in order to comment on the course of world history with an apocalyptically infused gloating, but in order to discover the sources of our modern fears. It may be that the archaic human being was always endangered by the feeling of an imminent end of his life and world, and we can see something of this also in our present fear of the nuclear catastrophe. But that is *ancient* fear, archaic fear. In my opinion, in modern man there is not primarily a fear that everything will come to an end, but more deeply rooted a fear that there will be no end at all, that our life and our history are pulled into the surging of a faceless evolution which finally rolls over us all as over grains of sand on the beach. This makes us powerless. Do not forget that the process of modern civilization and of modern science did not make people powerful; it has been a process of the humiliation of the subject. Today's critique of religion is not pointing to religion as an underestimation of human beings but as an irrational overestimation of human identity. It was Freud who spoke of a threefold humiliation of the human being by the processes of modern civilization: the humiliation of the Copernican revolution, saying that man's earth is not at the center of the cosmos; the revolution of Darwin, saying that the history of the human race is not at the center of the processes in the world but is just a very small, irrational piece; and Freud's own discovery that our consciousness is just a small drop in the sea of unconsciousness. We have to be aware of that. That is why I am pointing to what I call the pathology of modern mentalities, and why theology has to be aware of what I call the lack of great visions today. There are no longer great visions in our societies, either Eastern or Western. And what I admire in your president is that he was able to tell people that his politics was guided by a vision. I do not think that it is, but people at least understand it that way. Or consider the Marxist countries. What happened to Marxism in the socialist countries? It came down to a totalitarian bureaucracy. But that is not inherent in any one particular political system; it is the late metaphysics of modernity, as I understand it. (This is what I call the "ant mentality" of human people: the lack of resistance, playing possum in the face of danger, which makes us spectators of our own downfall in the face of the nuclear threat.) As far as I can see, the danger of the nuclear collapse of the world, of our earth — it is not a collapse of the world, since even after a nuclear disaster the processes will go on (without human beings, of course). We know we are included in such a subjectless history, but it makes us powerless. We are no longer able to think of an end of history. And I would say that the nuclear threat as such is not the danger, but rather the attitudes with which we encounter it. (Most of us are voyeurs, and it is very difficult to make people resist, to give them a mentality of resistance and to tell them that they should give up their mentality of being just helpless spectators of their own fate. It is a new kind of posthistoricity. Short-term strategies rule our public life instead of long-term strategies. We cultivate the art of alibi, the development of excuse mechanisms. Don't get involved too much! Think of yourself!)

There is a cult today of the makeable: everything can be made. There is also a new cult of fate: everything can be replaced. The will to make is undermined by resignation. The cult of the omnipotent control of man's destiny on the one hand and the cult of apathy on the other belong together like two sides of the same coin. The human understanding of reality, which guides our scientific and technical control of nature and from which the cult of the makeable draws its strength, is marked by an idea of time as a continuous process which is empty, surprise-free, and evolving toward infinity and within which everything is enclosed without grace. This understanding of reality and time excludes all expectation and therefore produces that fatalism that eats away man's soul. Man therefore is already resigned even before society has been able to introduce him successfully to this resignation as a form of so-called pragmatic rationality. This understanding of time generates that secret fear of identity which can be deciphered only with great difficulty because it is successfully practiced under the ciphers of progress and development before we may, just for a fleeting moment, discover it at the base of our souls. This is what I call the hermeneutics of danger, on the basis of a kind of naiveté.

The apocalyptic texts speak of the end of time and of history; they bring the cessation of these very near. But one has to look at these texts and images very carefully. They do not contain idle speculation about the date of a catastrophe, but rather a figurative commentary on the catastrophic and surprising nature of time itself. From the subversive viewpoint of the apocalyptic, time itself is full of hazard, danger, and surprise. It is not simply the evolutionarily stretched and empty eternity without surprises, into which we can project our progress without opposition. Time belongs not to Prometheus or to Faust, but to God. For the apocalyptic perspective, God is the mystery not yet brought forth, the mystery-in-waiting, of time. God is not seen as the "beyond" of time, but rather as its pressing end, its border, its salvific cessation. That is so because time, from the viewpoint of apocalyptic, is primarily a time of suffering — suffered time. The apocalyptic view subordinates without much ado natural time to the passiontide of humanity. For apocalyptic, a knowledge of identity is announced in the experience of human suffering, an identity which fiercely resists being reduced to the trivial identity of continuance over natural time. The continuity of time for apocalyptic is not the empty continuum of a modern understanding of time, but rather the trail of suffering. And the respect for the worth of suffering which accumulates in time impels apocalyptic to understand natural time from the viewpoint of suffered time, and thus to understand evolution from the viewpoint of history and indeed not to ignore the billions of years of natural time in relation to the time of the suffering of humanity, but to assess those eons as a kind of "inflated time" (as my old Marxist friend Ernst Bloch said).

But do we not all live and feel this way? Who relates his lifetime to the billions of years of evolutionary time? Who judges or appraises his action accordingly? Are we, therefore, all trapped in a gracious illusion — some because they refuse to give up an eschatological hope, as we do; others because they will not vindicate their fears? Or is there an as-yet-undisclosed, suppressed truth in the apocalyptic images?

From Holderlin we have the often-quoted phrase, "Where the danger is, there also grows the possibility of rescue." ("Wo die Gefahr ist, wachst das Rettende auch.") The apocalyptic reversal of this phrase would be, "When the possibility of rescue is near, then the danger grows." ("Wo die Rettung naht, wachst auch die Gefahr.") The vision of rescue or salvation as it shines from the biblical stories is not without an eschatological dialectic. This implies a final statement. Whenever Christianity becomes more and more domiciled and so more and more domesticated, whenever it becomes just the symbolic paraphrase of what would happen in any case, its messianic future becomes weak. Whenever Christianity seems hard to take, shrewish, and promising more danger than security, more homelessness than safety, it is close to him of whom it was said, "Who is close to me is close to the fire; who is far from me is far from the Kingdom." Only if we recognize something of the situation of our own Christian hope — our eschatological hope — in the apocalyptic symbols of danger, of crises and downfall, the images and symbols of the Kingdom will not decay like wishful thinking. (Only when we remain faithful to the symbols of the crisis can the symbols of promise and consolation remain faithful to us: the images and symbols of the great peace, of the home, of the Father, and of the kingdom of freedom, justice, and reconciliation, the images of the tears wiped away, and the images of the laughter of the children of God.)

Chapter 12

The Second Coming

No doubt an objection will be made to what I have said about following Christ and the demands this puts on us of poverty, celibacy, and obedience, and about the consequent demands that have been made of the religious orders: that this is an exorbitant and abstract request, beyond human endurance and just unlivable. To that I can only say: Yes, that is quite right. Following Christ when understood radically, that is, when grasped at the roots, is not livable — "if the time be not shortened" or, to put it another way, "if the Lord does not come soon." Without the expectation of the speedy coming of the Lord, following Christ cannot be lived; and without the hope of a shortening of the time it cannot be endured. Following Christ and looking forward to the second coming belong together like the two sides of a coin. His call to follow him and our plea, "Come, Lord Jesus," are inseparable. The testament of the early Church, which committed itself to the demands of the radical following of Christ, has a purpose in ending with the plea, "Maranatha, come, Lord Jesus."

Following Christ is not something that can be lived without the idea of the parousia, without looking forward to the second coming. Anyone who forgets this destroys following Christ or is engaged in silently destroying and mutilating it, since he cannot repeat actions that are always similar with the same intensity. What corresponds to following Christ is an existence based absolutely on hope: a life with an apocalyptic goad.

But surely we Christians offer the world a painful spectacle: that of people who talk about hope but really no longer look forward to anything. Is the Christian life still burdened with expectations and longings that are really part and parcel of a certain time? Do Christians — including members of religious orders — still really look forward to the end in, as it were, a state of tension? Do they look forward to an end at all — not just for themselves in the catastrophe of individual death but for the world and its time? Is a limitation and an end of time still conceivable — or has the expectation of an end of time not long since been banished to the realm of mythology, because time itself has become a homogeneous continuum free of surprise? Perhaps it has become mere unendingness: an empty eternity stretched out and dissolved by evolution in which anything and everything can happen except this one thing — that one particular second "should become the gateway through which the Messiah of history steps"[1] and in which it therefore becomes time for time's sake.

In the interval the symbols for the understanding of time have changed. The Christian apocalyptic symbol of time coming to an abrupt end has been exchanged for the crypto-religious symbol of evolution. That has penetrated all of us in its very impenetrability, right to the last glimmer of awareness, to such an extent that we hardly notice any longer its irrational sway over us and its quasi-religious totality. To prevent a current misunderstanding, and one that is given support in church circles, I should add that it is not really the temporal symbol of revolution but that of evolution that radically contradicts the Christian apocalyptic understanding of time, and that in people's minds has bred the special form of lack of expectation, the form of resignation and apathy, that today people like to call "rational," "sensible," and "pragmatic."

I think that theology and piety long ago surrendered to the anonymous pressure of this evolutionary awareness that owes far more to Descartes and Darwin than to the messianic awareness of time shown by the Bible. Do Christians still understand something that genuine piety has always understood, that is still apparent, for instance in Roger Schutz's words: "Prayer is primarily waiting: awaiting. It means letting the 'Come, Lord' of the Apocalypse rise up in oneself day by day. Come for mankind, come for me myself?"[2] Is this still realized at all, let alone the idea that a person should fearfully ask himself whether the only reason the Lord does not come is perhaps because the longing for him has not been strong enough, not mystically deep enough, and not politically real enough?

We have to ask whether theology has not long been able to make sense of anything and everything without an awareness of an end to time (even if the Lord does not come). For if I see things correctly, all the predominant varieties of contemporary eschatology — those hinged on the present just as much as those hinged on the future — have already successfully adjusted to an evolutionary understanding of time that is alien to them. They have accepted an understanding that compels them to make all expectation of the second coming an extremely private concern, focused on the death of the individual, and that obliges them either to think of God's future strictly without reference to time or to project it into a pattern of evolution. Surely theology long ago adopted an awareness of time that allows it to understand itself as a kind of institutionally pro-

---

1. The phrase is borrowed from Walter Benjamin.
2. Cf. Roger Schutz, *Ein Fest ohne Ende* (Gütersloh, 1977), 44.

tected permanent reflection, not stimulated by any imminent expectation of the second coming, uninterrupted by any awareness of catastrophe, hence lacking the urgency imposed both by time and by action, and appallingly scared of contact with any definite pattern of behavior? The reinterpretation of the imminent expectation of the second coming as continual expectation and the way in which this made the political factor a matter of indifference remain an objective (if semantic) betrayal of the temporal basis of Christian hope.

There is a final problem that concerns the whole of the life of the Church. The Church seems to have the overwhelming effect of an institution that suppresses expectations that can be disappointed (the genuine ones) and replaces them with a more stable alternative: purely individual, timeless hopes. Does it not, like every other institution, function as an antiapocalyptic establishment that in the name of proportion and balance, of feasible popular demands, has long offered the excesses and exaggerations of Christianity at reasonable prices, compounded with the course of events, without having to count on the speedy return of its Lord? Yet following Christ and the imminent expectation of his second coming belong so closely together that one cannot more or less completely cancel or surrender one of them without compromising the other and then losing it altogether.

A passionate protest is needed against the lack of expectation in our ecclesiastical and religious life. The Church needs something like an apocalyptic shock that cannot be prescribed for it by official theological circles. Nor will it be contributed by sectarian zealots. The shock effect must be produced inside the Church by those who are open to what is outside the Church and what lies on its fringe, and who are capable of the fearless discernment of spirits: those who commit themselves so consistently to following Christ that they are forced on to the side of those who mourn in human history and human society.

The passionate expectation of the day of the Lord does not lead to an apocalyptic reverie in which all the practical demands entailed by following Christ are forgotten and evaporate. Nor does it impel one into an unthinking radicalism for which prayers of longing and expectation can only be forms of refusal or self-deception that have been shown up as such. Following Christ on the basis of imminent expectation of the second coming averts the danger of an ineffectual state of permanent reflection. The kind of following we want does not merely reflect itself but impels one toward action and forbids any postponement of following Christ. The well-known last judgment discourse of Matthew 25 — where the king separates the just from the unjust according to the criterion: "As you did it (or did it not) to one of the least of these my brethren, you did it (or did it not) to me" — is thoroughly apocalyptic in character, since awareness of the end and of the judgment is linked in it with the idea of the necessity of active commitment to others, for "the least of the brethren." To live Christian hope on the basis of imminent expectation of the second coming does not mean sacrificing its social and political responsibility but the reverse: injecting the urgency imposed by time and the need to act into a responsibility that has been robbed of its tension by extending the expectation of the second coming to infinity — one that has been diluted and deferred. "In all these experiences and encounters [in the countries of the Third World] I am continually overcome by a concerned feeling of urgency," Father Arrupe said recently.

> Do not we Christians hesitate too much and too long? Are not our plans often too long-term and do they not play safe too much? Surely we stick too readily to what is guaranteed and tested, and our courage deserts us too rapidly when we face open-ended and risk ventures. I do not want here to speak up for aimless panic. But if according to Scripture we are called on to read the signs of the times, then included in that today is essentially a feeling for the closeness of our deadlines and a readiness to act quickly.[3]

Imminent expectation of the second coming repairs hope that has been soothed and led astray by ideas of evolution. It offers hope the perspectives of expectation and time. It does not paralyze responsibility but gives it a solid foundation.

There is a possible misunderstanding here. The idea of apocalyptic has not been introduced more or less fortuitously. It is of no use for filling gaps in a chain of reasoning — for example, in the theology of following Christ. Nor should it ever become mere playing with theological concepts or pure speculation. Whenever it has exhausted itself in number games and advance calculations about the history of salvation it has done so because it was already worn out and degenerate. Apocalypse is and must remain the mystical counterpart of a lived political reality. What this political reality is is apparent from the history of religion and particularly the New Testament. Times of crisis, when people suffer persecution and when injustice and inhumanity have reached massive proportions, inspire and drive forward the pious and devoted toward apocalyptic longing.

Perhaps the reason why our age produces no apocalyptic prophets and apocalyptic language seems out of place is that this age and its crises, catastrophes, injustices, and examples of inhumanity dispense the sweet poison of evolutionary progress and — despite everything — the illusion

---

3. From an address he gave in the Paulskirche at Frankfurt in 1976.

of incessant growth, and thus make everyone insensible and unreceptive to the real extent of anxiety. Apocalyptic experience is not so out of tune with the times as it can appear to most people. But what is meant by saying *it is time* in a time for which it will never really be time?

"It is time for it to be time. It is time," the poet Paul Celan wrote. It is precisely this antievolutionary consciousness, one out of tune with the times, that the present time calls for. And if this apocalyptic awareness were to emerge in the religious orders, and were given a stable form under the influence of following Christ (even though that is hardly livable), then today would indeed be the age, the time, the moment of the religious orders — that would also be true in regard to the life of society in general.

What is at the bottom of the modern awareness that we call reasonable and practical? Is it not a special apathy and lack of expectation that continually leads one astray and toward successful adaptation to the status quo, to a lack of resistance to the way of the world, to passivity to those who set themselves up as rulers of the age? Surely the idea of time as something evolutionary and unending has long since bred in people's minds a special form of resignation that persists long after it has been labeled "science," "objectivity," and "pragmatism." Our modern world with its civilization based on science and technology is not just a rational universe. Its myth is evolution. The concealed concern of its rationality is the fiction that time is an empty infinity without surprises. Its eschaton is boredom and apathy. The corresponding social signs are difficult to overlook. What we have is

> in the West a pluralist boredom that depends on free enterprise and in the East a monolithic boredom that depends on orders and oppression.... It all looks as it does during a partial eclipse of the sun: everything is so strangely grey, and the birds either do not sing at all or sing differently. So something is afoot. Transcendent reality is weak.[4]

This menacing age is, if possible, the age of the religious orders, the age of those whose aim it is publicly to reject all adaptation and those who by a rigorous and uncompromising way of life try to protect themselves from manipulation. I would in any case be disappointed if their apocalyptic protest, which is stressed to the point of having a distinctive garb, were to have declined to mere ritual and ultimately a gesture of flight from social responsibility.

---

4. The wording is Ernst Bloch's.

It is the age of the religious orders in a peculiarly apocalyptic sense. This applies especially to the life of the Church today. The synod document *Our Hope* says:

> The way of the Church is the way of lived hope. It is also the law of all church renewal. And it leads us to the only answer that ultimately we can give to all doubts and disappointments, all rejection and all indifference. Are we what we acknowledge in the witness of our hope? Is our church life characterized by the spirit and the power of this hope? A church that adapts itself to this hope is finally adapted also to the present day, and without adaptation to this hope no *aggiornamento*, however powerful it may potentially be, can help it. "The world" does not need religion to redouble its lack of hope: what it needs and is looking for, if it is doing so at all, is the counterweight, the explosive force of lived hope. And what we owe it is this: to balance the deficit of hope that is seen to be lived. In this sense the question about our responsibility to and our significance for the present is finally the same as that about our identity as Christians: are we what we acknowledge in the witness of our hope?

Who can ensure that these words become endurable and acceptable to the people of this age who lack hope and expectation, so that they do not sound like fairytales from the past nor like the out-of-date ideology of a Church that has adapted too well to the society in which it lives?

An age of the religious orders? This is a question that must, above all, be directed to the Church, which needs apocalyptic men and women who demonstrate the radical nature of Christian hope before people's eyes in a way that cannot be overlooked. They must do so not in order to relieve ordinary Christians of the burden of this radical nature but to bind the whole Church plainly to the demands of the creed it proclaims.

The synod document ends by putting things distinctly in an apocalyptic perspective that clearly emphasizes this obligation: "All our initiatives are ultimately measured by the standard of 'the one hope that belongs to your call' " (Eph. 4:4). Hope does not spring out of the unknown or impel us into what is accidental. It has its roots in Christ, and even among us Christians of the late twentieth century it demands the expectation of his second coming. It is continually turning us into people who in the middle of their historical experience and struggles lift up their heads and look toward the messianic "day of the Lord":

> Then I saw a new heaven and a new earth;...and I heard a great voice from the throne saying, "Behold, the dwelling of God is with

men. He will dwell with them, and they shall be his people, and God himself will be with them; he will wipe away every tear from their eyes, and death shall be no more, neither shall there be mourning nor crying nor pain any more...." And he who sat upon the throne said, "Behold, I make all things new." (Rev. 21:1, 3–5)

Chapter 13

The Courage to Pray

Many people today no longer pray even in private. Prayer seems strange, alienating, and inaccessible. We feel no inclination for it even when prayer is the only form of language that can express our lives and feelings adequately. Surely no Christian nowadays would dispute that we need the courage to pray, especially for ourselves.

The Historical Solidarity of Prayer

To begin, I should like to discuss the historical solidarity of those who pray. We are not alone when we pray; we have more support than most of us realize. We are part of a great tradition which has formed our identity as human beings. This tradition stretches right back to the unknown beginnings of the history of mankind. As the German Synod text *Our Hope* says, "The name of God is graven deeply in the history of mankind's hopes and sufferings. It brings enlightenment and is obscured, is revered and denied, misused and disgraced, yet never forgotten."

What do we know about the history of mankind? First and foremost we know something about the great and the mighty, about the rulers and their victories, and sometimes about their tragedies. In the past those were the facts that shaped our knowledge of history. But what about the others, the countless masses who actually won the victories for their rulers, who built the monuments and who mourned their numerous dead? What do we know about them? One thing we can say with certainty is that in their suffering and their grief, in their joy and their fear, they called to God, imploring him and admonishing him, praising him and thanking him. They prayed. Their history is the history of prayer.

The history of mankind seen as popular history is basically the history of religion, and religious history in the final analysis is the history of prayer. And this is not limited to the history of Christian Europe. It applies especially to Judeo-Hebraic history, which in turn became the foundation of history for both Christianity and Islam. It applies equally to many remote, impenetrable cultures in Asia and Africa. We Christians

157

should have every respect for this unfamiliar history and for the validity of the hopes and sufferings it contains.

(Through prayer we become part of a great historical solidarity. Prayer introduces into the history of mankind a voice that gives expression to our hope and trust.) Yet the significance of this religious voice throughout the history of mankind, this silent plea for prayer from the anonymous mass of the dead, is frequently disputed. The concept of the history of mankind as the history of mankind at prayer has often been disregarded or dismissed. The dead are easily overlooked. Perhaps our attitude to the history of prayer is determined by sympathy rather than respect. We make excuses for it instead of taking it seriously: "They didn't know any better; they had a false consciousness; they still lived in a collective darkness conditioned by archaic fears. . . . Most of them were frankly credulous. But their voices cannot be included in the present dispute about humanity and its hopes. The ignorant have no competence to speak." To decide who is knowledgeable and who is ignorant with respect to hope, religion, and prayer is not a matter for those who have themselves lived and suffered in the light of religious experience; nor can it be decided by those who pray, the subjects of this language of prayer. Instead, the decision lies with those of us who adhere to the idea of a logical evaluation of mankind, invariably equating knowledge with more recent stages of development, and thus reducing earlier ages to the level of mass ignorance. This attitude accounts for the long-established practice of harshly and mindlessly criticizing and destroying the memories and symbols of this history of prayer. This can take many forms: through writing (a focus of apathy); in the easy comfort of lengthy reflection, protected from the irritating limitations of practical application; in the "safe" realm of pure theory, well insulated against any apocalyptical storm, yet aware of everything, with nothing strange or unexplained, where all languages are known and spoken, with the exception of the language of suffering and hope, which is prayer.

If we are to avoid succumbing to the current illusion which equates the present with the most advanced state of human awareness, we must remind ourselves that the sum total of the living is far too small, too arbitrary, and probably also too lacking in imagination, and hence is not competent to make any final judgment about the fate of religion and prayer. Should we not therefore be more willing to extend the right to a say in matters of religion and prayer to include the dead also? Surely we must discard any superficial impression that prayer is too weak or insipid if it requires the support of the dead and the voice of tradition in order to survive.

Those who pray are part of a great historical company. The chief mainstay of this solidarity is, above all, the history of prayer contained in the Old Testament, and indeed that of the Jewish people. This is not without contemporary relevance, for example, in the case of Germany. Referring to the Nazi concentration camps a Jewish philosopher coined the well-known saying that after Auschwitz poetry was dead. And what about prayer? Can we take it for granted that after Auschwitz it is still possible to pray? A Marxist philosopher of religion, Milan Machoveč, felt strongly that it was not. During a debate in 1966 he asked me how, after Auschwitz, Christians still found the courage to pray. The answer I tried to give him still strikes me as the only convincing one: "We can and should pray after Auschwitz because even in Auschwitz, in the hell of Auschwitz, they prayed." This context links prayer in Germany, for instance, in a very special way with the history of prayer of the Jewish people. And it is an indication of the promise *and* the obligation implied in the opening words of this chapter: Those who pray are not alone; they form part of a great historical company; prayer is a matter of historical solidarity.

What Is Prayer?

But what is prayer? I should like to comment on the *characteristics* of prayer and the *language* of prayer. Again, it is not my intention to say much "about" prayer as such — how could one say everything that would need to be said? Rather, I wish to give people encouragement to pray.

To pray is to say "Yes" to God, to affirm the sense of contradiction we experience, the pain of mortality and death, the suffering caused by violence and oppression.

> I am overcome by my trouble. I am distraught by the noise of the enemy, because of the oppression of the wicked....My heart is in anguish within me, the terrors of death have fallen upon me. Fear and trembling come upon me, and horror overwhelms me. And I say, "O that I had wings like a dove!" ...But I call upon God; and the Lord will save me. (Psalm 55)

This psalm shows that our simple definition of prayer is full of tension and drama. In no way is the difficulty of saying "Yes" concealed or glossed over with false confidence. The great tradition of prayer in the Old Testament — in the psalms, in Job, in the lamentations of the prophets — makes it clear that the language of prayer does not exclude or shut itself off from the experience of suffering and desolation. On the contrary, it is the language of pain and crisis, of lament and accusation; it is the grumbling and outcry of the children of Israel. "Therefore I will not restrain my mouth; I will speak in the anguish of my spirit; I will complain in the bitterness of my soul" (Job 7). The language of prayer is that of our impassioned questioning of God and hence also expresses our tensely anxious expectation that God will one day vindicate the terrible suffering of the world. Protest is fused with unreserved lament, and the tenderness of the language in no way denies its sadness.

The language of prayer does not express joy either patronizingly or peremptorily. Nor is it submissive like the language of a servant to his master. Those who pray are certainly neither weak yes-men nor bound by compulsive obedience; they are neither cowards nor piously subservient. The very nature of the language of prayer throughout the Old Testament contradicts that attitude.

Again and again prayer is a cry of lament from the depths of the spirit. But this cry is in no sense a vague, rambling moan. It calls out loudly, insistently. Nor is it merely a wish or a desire, no matter how fervent. It is a supplication. The language of prayer finds its purpose and justification in the silently concealed face of God. Hence the lament, supplication, crying, and protest contained in prayer, as also the silent accusation of the wordless cry, can never simply be translated and dissolved into a discourse.

Precisely because it cannot be translated, the language of prayer is so comprehensive and liberating. No other form of language is so free from linguistic constraints. Nothing is excluded, be it doubt, resignation, protest, or rejection, provided that the individual wishes to turn to God and to seek his confidence. We can tell God everything: all our suffering, our doubt, even our doubt about our faith in him and about his hearing us when we turn to him. In this sense the Old Testament language of prayer is full of formulations somewhat daunting to the ordinary Christian. In fact they demonstrate that these prayers are alive. Prayer does not restrain or constrain the language of suffering; rather it extends it immeasurably, ineffably.

Christian prayer should always retain this quality. Christians have all too frequently given the impression that their religion is based on a plethora of answers and too few impassioned questions. But Christianity is much more than a religion of dogmas. And Christian prayer is certainly not a game of questions and answers. We need only to look at Jesus and his prayer to see this. Jesus' prayer, very briefly, culminates in his cry to the Father for having forsaken him. The degree of acquiescence and obedience contained in this cry reflects the measure of his suffering. His suffering came from God. His prayer from the cross is the cry of one forsaken by God, yet of one who has never deserted God. This suffering is different again from the expression of solidarity with the misery of the world. There is nothing noble about this suffering, nothing of the sublimity of love that must suffer impotently. In the words of the Bible, it is the suffering of the desolate. This is the spirit in which Jesus says "Yes" and dies in affirmation. The mysticism of suffering embodied in the prayers of the Old Testament is not suppressed or diminished. On the contrary it is grasped at its very roots.

Approaches to Prayer

Prayer is not a desperate attempt to pull ourselves out of the abyss. We gain the strength to pray from Christ's prayer. "Following in the steps of Jesus we must live according to the poverty of his obedience. Through prayer we dare to offer our lives unconditionally to the Father." At this point I should like to comment on the different approaches to this kind of prayer.

There is, for example, the *prayer of fear*. Praying is not an imaginary ladder enabling us to escape from our fears. Nor does it suppress or overcome our fears. First and foremost it permits fear. "My soul is very sorrowful, even to death," Christ prayed in the Garden of Gethsemane (cf. Matt. 26:38). Fear is allowed in, not banished. Fear, sorrow, and distress can easily provide the impetus to pray. Apathy has no part to play in prayer. The aim of prayer is not to protect us from pain or suffering. Nothing alarms us more than a person ostensibly devoid of fear. But is it not true that fear makes people malleable and unfree; that frightened people are precisely those most liable to be exploited by outside forces? We must be more specific. Only when fear is suppressed do we become unfree and manipulated; only then can fear constrict our hearts and render us incapable of conceiving our own anguish or that of those around us. By means of prayer, however, this fear can even make us free, just as Christ was freed by his fearful prayer of distress in the Garden of Olives.

Then there is *prayer induced by guilt*. Again prayer can prevent us from giving in to the web of excuses we weave around ourselves; it can help us cope with the misery of our guilty consciences. What can we feel if, reflecting on the past, we have to admit to ourselves that our lives are scattered with the ruins of people destroyed by our egoism? Faced with such a realization, what reaction could we have but an overwhelming desire to make amends? What alternative is there to despair but the plea for forgiveness and, according to the messianic light of hope, additional pleas precisely for those destroyed? This argument is, of course, open to the suspicion that our religious outcry in reaction to our own guilt amounts to a very subtle form of escapism, both from ourselves and from responsibility. I shall return later to the idea that prayer incorporates the readiness to accept responsibility. At this point I should like to draw attention to a number of ways of approaching the mystical aspect of prayer.

The examples given above might possibly suggest that the way to prayer is through negative experiences, through pain, sorrow, and distress, rather than through the positive influence of joy and gratitude. In reality, however, the active fight against overwhelming hopelessness, affirmation in the negative face of pain, is the outcome of a tremendously positive attitude. The experience of prayer I wish to underline here has a long tradition in the history of religion and especially in the history of our own faith. In history prayer is not limited to the expression of joy and exaltation; on the contrary, it also embraces the expression of fear and despair, a cry from the depths of the soul.

For this reason I should like to mention a danger which I feel is implicit in the customary language of prayer currently used by the Church. Perhaps not enough emphasis is laid on the pain of negativity? Perhaps our prayers are often much too positive and overaffirmative, resorting to clichés when referring to suffering and conflict and thus incapable of giving adequate expression to our acceptance of difficulties and crises? In my view this kind of prayer is symptomatic of weakness and despondency, and no longer entrusts our pain and the despair of our lives to God in prayer.

This tendency to be overly affirmative in our daily prayers is full of serious implications. It surely exacerbates our inarticulateness in pain and crises, depressing us further instead of giving us courage. How can people in dangerous situations, in pain or oppression, identify with prayers which use this kind of language? And how can this language be combined with those "traces of prayer" which can still be found even in our so-called postreligious age? I mean here the powerless rebellion against overwhelming meaninglessness, the lament and elegy which manage to survive in spite of the suppression of sadness and melancholy in contemporary society, and the cry for justice for unexpiated suffering.

It is precisely because of this absence of suffering in the official Christian language of prayer that we generally fail to notice what "modern humanity" loses with the gradual impoverishment of the language of prayer. The disappearance of this language of prayer means, in the most literal sense, that we have lost the only language capable of expressing many situations and experiences in our lives.

Prayer and Politics

At this point I must turn to the *purpose and function of prayer* "in the spirit of Christ." The underlying mysticism of this kind of prayer is evident. It entails a shift in responsibility, both social and political. "Christ's obedience is also the source of his particular love for mankind, his closeness to the humble, the rejected, the sinners and the desolate" (from the German Synod text *Our Hope*).

solidarity

If we are to pray "in the spirit of Christ" we cannot turn our backs on the sufferings of others. Prayer demands that we love our fellow humans; we have no choice. It can make prayer extremely dangerous, for example, in situations where humanity is systematically suppressed and people are forced to live as though no bonds of allegiance existed between them. This need for humanity urges Christians today to adopt a positive attitude toward prayer. We must pray not just *for* the poor and unfortunate but *with* them. This contradicts our instinctive tendency to avoid the company of those who are unhappy or suffering. If we pray "in his spirit" we can afford to be despised by those who consider themselves to be intelligent and enlightened; but not by those who are disconsolate, suffering, or oppressed. And this means that prayer is of necessity political and influential.

Hence we must take care not to let our prayers turn into a eulogistic evasion of what really matters, serving merely to lift the apathy from our souls and our indifference and lack of sympathy toward other people's suffering. Let us consider the language of our "modern" prayers of petition which often purport to be "explicit" and "social" in intent. Are they really prayers or merely excuses by which we take the easy option, with little risk of responsibility? "Lord, help drug addicts back to a 'normal' life" or "Lord, help prevent racial discrimination, and give food to the poor countries of the Third World." Surely the only practical effect of such prayers can be to appease our consciences. A mature attitude toward prayer presupposes the readiness to assume responsibility. And it feeds on the contradictory, painful feelings which necessarily accompany the acceptance and fulfillment of this responsibility.

This practical and political aspect of prayer is also highly relevant in a religious sense. We should face up to our fears and doubts and consider in all seriousness the nature of the God to whom we direct our prayers. Is this silent, faceless God not an indifferent idol, a Baal, a Moloch? Is he not an unbearable tyrant enthroned in an elevated realm to which our longings and sufferings have no entry? Is he not the reflection and sealing of a feudalistic master-slave relationship, the last remnant of an obsolete, archaic system of sovereignty? Perhaps the mysticism of prayer leads to misanthropic masochism? Surely prayer poisons our hard-won freedom of consciousness with further archaic fears and constraints? With such questions in mind it is important to study the prayers of Christ himself. The God of his prayers is "our Father," too; his prayers, his whole de-

meanor, his entire destiny make this evident. From this we can see clearly
that the God of his prayers is neither a humiliating tyrant nor the projection of worldly power and authority. Rather, he is the God of insuperable
love, the God of a dwelling almost beyond our imagining, the God who
wipes away our tears and gathers lost souls into the radiant clasp of his
mercy. Hence as followers of Christ we must continually make it clear,
both to ourselves and to others, to whom we are praying and whom we
mean when we say "God." (The qualities of this liberating, edifying God
to whom we pray must be visible in our conduct and attitudes.) There can
be no universally effective theoretical contradiction of the suspicion that
prayer is the opium of the people, or indeed that it is intended specifically
for the people and is the classical expression of a false consciousness.
Nor can we successfully use "pure theory" to counter attempts to de-
prive prayer of its authenticity by adapting it to the functional systems
of a liberal society, treating it as a welcome means of absorbing socially
generated disappointments and frustrations: in short, regarding prayer
as a useful social tool to ensure the smooth running of society. The only
effective stand we can take against such attacks is to be active followers
of Christ, who in his prayers called God his "Father" and ours.

Prayer as Meditation

What does prayer remind us of? The answer, perhaps surprisingly, is
that prayer reminds us of *ourselves*. This is all the odder, given that we
spend more and more time trying to forget ourselves. Because of the
highly complex, largely anonymous social systems in which we live there
is a real danger of our identity being lost, of our dreams and fantasies
being reduced to nothing, of our being reduced to the level of expedient
animals and machines functioning smoothly in the name of evolution and
technology. This so-called progress surely has a very damaging effect on
what we call our self-awareness. We feel powerless in the face of a grimly
sinister universe, and drawn into an anonymous evolution which engulfs
each of us mercilessly. "As for man, his days are like grass; he flourishes
like a flower of the field; for the wind passes over it, and it is gone, and
its place knows it no more" (Psalm 103). What we are undergoing today
is surely an extension on a universal scale of this experience from the
nomadic world of the Old Testament. At the same time our primitive fear
of losing our name is also increasing. Thus we can see the contemporary
relevance of the Old Testament prayer: "The Lord called me from the
womb, from the body of my mother he named my name" (Isa. 49:1). In
saying "Yes" to God we are reminded of ourselves. Prayer is the oldest
form of the human battle for subjectivity and identity against all odds.

Prayer reminds us in particular of *childhood.* It is like returning to our
own childhood, to its feeling of confidence but also to its unanswered
questions and longings. Somehow prayer always retains the difficulties
of childhood. Yet this childlike quality reveals that the spontaneity of
prayer has as little to do with artificial or dubious naiveté as it has with
spontaneous existential optimism. In this context I should like to risk
adapting a famous phrase of Ernst Bloch's (stemming originally, he has
stated, from an ancient Indian tradition) to prayer: Prayer is at times like
the daydream of that home whose light shines in our childhood, yet a
home where none of us has ever been.

Prayer as Resistance

Finally, I wish to consider what prayer is *reacting against:* to see prayer
as an alternative attitude in our personal and daily lives. Prayer is really
an act of opposition.

Prayer opposes the threatening banality of our lives. It resists the de-
basement of human life to a society focused on needs and consumerism,
in which the ability to mourn and to celebrate declines because needs
can only be fulfilled, not celebrated, and because mourning is quite literally valueless. Prayer, as stressed previously, is not a question-and-answer
game; nor is it to be seen as barter. God does speak, but be does not give
answers and almost never repeats himself. Prayer makes our questions
seem questionable; it alienates our wishes; it reassesses our interests. It
removes us from the vicious circle of question and answer, of means
and end.

Prayer is an assault on the prevailing apathy with which we consistently and increasingly protect ourselves against hurt and disappointment
until we finally reach the stage where nothing can touch us anymore. In
the face of these widespread identity fears I see a new stoicism emerging
which, in order to avoid having to experience pain, refuses to acknowledge life as a struggle. Insensibility will be the rubric of this new cult.
(Apathy far more than hatred has a destructive effect on religion and
prayer. It is also worse for oneself and for one's future in a human society
based on freedom and solidarity. The moderate feelings of our day-to-
day existence can scarcely be of any help here. We need to be stirred up
by more extreme emotions: we need a prayer that embodies these feelings, that does not suppress them in any way but activates them against
the gradual dominance of apathy. (It is bad enough that our traditional
form of prayer has not really evolved a language suitable to express this.
For example, where would we find language of mourning in which the
mourner does not deny his grief, but rather expresses it himself?)

In the final analysis prayer is a resistance to that particular kind of hopelessness and resignation which takes root in our highly developed consciousness no matter how often we dismiss it rationally or pragmatically. This hopelessness is exactly the right prerequisite for our kind of technically and pragmatically orientated rationality. Its calculating logic presupposes a concept of time as an endless, constant continuum. Perhaps the feeling of being locked into an infinite, empty, anonymous time — called "evolution" — has long since extinguished any substantial sense of hope or expectation. Do we still know what it means to wait in anticipation for something? Not for the individual at a given time in the world, but for this time itself, for the world as a whole. All of us must surely have experienced this feeling. The radio announcer gives a brief, matter-of-fact report about some shattering catastrophe, and the music begins again. It is as though the music were an acoustic metaphor for the course of time, halted by nothing, submerging everything mercilessly and endlessly. Or can we see it differently?

(Prayer is a source of opposition, an "intermission," a means of resistance to that inexorable continuity which reduces us to apathy and makes us so apolitical (as will be borne out by the technocratic future of our societies), and so makes us incapable of expecting anything) Samuel Beckett's *Waiting for Godot* is not a play which would easily lend itself to a theological adaptation as an eschatological drama about the anticipation of God. It does not say anything about God, but in my view it does deal with "waiting," or rather with this epoch's "inability to anticipate or expect anything." Perhaps Christians have also drifted into this unfortunate state? "Again and again we continue to claim that we are waiting and watching for the Lord. But if we were honest with ourselves, we should have to admit that we no longer expect anything" (Teilhard de Chardin).

Prayer can and must be the source which renews this expectation. It must stir us up against that annihilating hopelessness which undermines any commitment based on an ulterior motive. Hence Christianity's oldest prayer is simultaneously the most up to date: "Come, Lord Jesus!" (Rev. 22:20).

Chapter 14

In the Pluralism of Religious and Cultural Worlds

Notes Toward a Theological and Political Program

The new political theology is the attempt to talk about the times, more precisely, to discuss the prevailing historical, social, and cultural situation so that the memory of God found in the biblical traditions might have a future. Therefore, one consistently finds in this theology the general markings ("signatures") of its starting point in the "discussions of the times." One speaks, for example, of "the time of a crisis of God," of "the age of cultural amnesia," and, in the light of these, of "the time of a fundamental pluralism" — all attempts to formulate theologically relevant labels for "the spiritual situation of the times" (Karl Jaspers).

I

We live in a time of fundamental pluralism — of cultures, of religions, of worldviews. Every attempt to question this pluralism is suspect. Universalism is regarded as latent imperialism and universal obligation as a deceptive intellectual and moral trap. The perception and safeguarding of difference and otherness is demanded and sought after — grounded in the (postmodern) sensitivity to the dangers lurking in universal concepts and their denigration of plurality and difference.

This crisis of traditional universal approaches in no way signals an end to questions about the relationship of "universalism and pluralism." In my view the most important question might be formulated in this way: Given the undeniable diversity of cultural and religious worlds, is there still a universally binding and thus plausible criterion for understanding? Or is everything now at the whim of the postmodern market? The era of postmodern fragmentation contains an ethical *aporia:* we live in a time

Translated by John Downey and Heiko Wiggers

in which the ethical problems of our scientific, technological, and economic civilization increasingly lay beyond the reach of the individual. Such problems can only be dealt with, if at all, under the rubric of politics and political ethics. Never before in the history of humankind has there been so broad and long-term a moral challenge. As never before, ethical concern is about the courage of "an ethics for the future" (Hans Jonas). At the same time, in our era of so-called globalization, any ethical universalism in behavior or action is suspected of being an antipluralistic moral totalitarianism.

Is there still such a thing as a moral universe that can be ethically described? How are the universalism of human rights and the notion of the inalienable and intrinsic cultural differences of humankind tied to one another? Must these two repeatedly relativize each other in a nonrelational, which is to say "noncommittal," diversity which leads again and again to new conflicts and eruptions of violence? Is there any criterion which can help us determine where the legitimate plurality of inculturated ethical approaches finds its limits? One can see the total inconsistency of the situation in Samuel Huntington's bestseller, *The Clash of Civilizations*.[1]

Huntington warns of universalizing, as he puts it, "Western values." But at the same time he also argues for something like a universal moral standard which, in the case of systematic abuse, might even require intervention. What is that about? What are the criteria and characteristics of such a universality?

We live, one might say, in a world of undeniable plurality. Tolerance, dialogue, and discourse are demanded. Certainly. But is this the entire answer? Are there not limits to tolerance and criteria for dialogue? And are there not also situations in which the formal, purely procedural rationality of discourse fails? Pluralism is not simply the answer, but first of all the question and the problem. To solve this problem doesn't mean to dissolve pluralism. The point is to develop a way of dealing with it that is open and reasonable to all, avoiding cultural relativism without simply relativizing and trivializing the cultures themselves.

What, however, would these "commonalities," these common goods, as they were once called, be? Today this commonality is largely denied and the few people who dare discuss universals in our radically pluralistic world are limited to a purely formal, purely procedural, supposedly context-free universalism. Is there then no inculturated ethic that can be

---

1. Samuel P. Huntington, *The Clash of Civilizations and the Remaking of World Order* (New York: Simon and Schuster, 1996). Though the question mark has now disappeared, the thesis was originally formulated in his "Clash of Civilizations?" *Foreign Affairs* 72 (1993): 21–29. For a recent critique of this "new global politics," see William Pfaff, "Huntington's Irrtum," in *Lettre International* (Summer 1997): 11–24.

universalized without violence, an ethic which doesn't destroy but protects the pluralism of our cultural life-worlds? Are there no guidelines for living and acting that spring from a historical tradition and could be regarded as universal or universalizable? Is this possible without being imperial or totalitarian, without ignoring the new sensitivity for plurality and indifference, for the otherness of the other, for their dignity and their claim?

The traditions and contexts of our religious and cultural worlds should be questioned and tested. I can only discuss this very briefly here. Today many people — especially in our Western cultural circles — favor a religion without God. Doesn't this appear to be a much "softer" and more tolerant religious paradigm for our age of radical pluralism? Isn't such a religion more compatible with pluralism and more appropriate than remembering the biblical God who, after all, has come down to us as the God of history and law? Nevertheless, my suggestion for reconciliation between a definite universality and an authentic plurality focuses on these very traditions. It concerns our memory of the God of the biblical traditions, a God whose memory comes to expression in the memory of human suffering. Further, it concerns our memory of the Christ of Christians as expressed in the historical memory of suffering, the *memoria passionis*. The cultic memory of the resurrection (the *memoria resurrectionis*) has been tied to our historical experience, preventing its being celebrated only as a myth far removed from history and responsibility. At first the suggestion to ground moral universalism in religious contexts sounds rather cryptic and tedious, especially if one wants to justify this suggestion not primarily religiously and politically, but — in the style of the new political theology — strictly theologically. What does this entail?

II

The biblical traditions know a particular type of universal responsibility. Certainly it must be carefully noted that the universalism of this responsibility is not primarily directed toward the universalism of sin and failure, but rather toward the universalism of suffering in the world. Jesus didn't look first to the sin of others but to the suffering of others. To him sin was, above all, a refusal to participate in the suffering of others, a refusal to see beyond one's own history of suffering. Sin was, as Augustine put it, turning the heart inward, surrendering to the furtive narcissism of the creature. And so Christianity began as a community of memory and narrative in imitation of Jesus, a community of those who looked first to the suffering of others.

This sensitivity to another's suffering, this taking into consideration the suffering of others, including that of enemies, in one's actions is the center of that "new way of life" tied to Jesus. It is, in my opinion, the most persuasive expression of that love which Jesus presumed and expected of us when — in accordance with his Jewish heritage — he called for the unity of love of God and love of neighbor.

The parables of Jesus have captured the human memory in a special way. Foremost among these parables is that of the Good Samaritan with which Jesus answers the question, "Who is my neighbor?" In our context, this is the question: For whom am I responsible? For whom am I to care? One thing becomes clear from this parable, told in images of an archaic provincial community: it is not up to us to define clearly and delimit in advance the range of this responsibility, the breadth of this caring. The "neighbor" and thus partner in our caring is never only the one whom we ourselves regard and accept as such. The range of this caring, the breadth of this responsibility is, in principle, unlimited. The criterion for its degree and scope is and remains the suffering of the other, as we see in Jesus' story about a man who falls in with robbers and whom the Priest and Levite pass by "out of a higher interest." People who use "God" the way Jesus does accept the violation of their own personal preconceived certainties by the misfortune of others. To speak of this God means to speak of the suffering of the stranger and to lament responsibility neglected and solidarity denied.

The appeal to a sensitivity to suffering in the biblical message, just as in the *memoria passionis* connected with it, is in no way marked by resignation or evasion. This appeal has nothing to do with a religiously motivated narcissism. After all, this *memoria passionis* is a memory of suffering which always takes into account the suffering of others, of strangers, and — according to the Bible — even the suffering of enemies. And this is not to be forgotten in our assessment of our personal history of suffering. This remembering the suffering of the other lies at the forefront of the political, social, and cultural conflicts of today's world. In the face of the widening gap between the rich and the poor and of the promising exchange between cultural and religious worlds, voicing the suffering of others is the absolute prerequisite for any future politics of peace, for any new forms of social solidarity.

(In the former Yugoslavia the memory of suffering became a shroud for a whole nation and a stranglehold on any attempt at interethnic rapprochement. Here a particular people have remembered only their own suffering, and so this purely self-regarding *memoria passionis* became not an organ of understanding and peace, but a source of hostility, hatred, and violence.) The present situation between Israel and the Palestinians is, one still hopes, different. There remains for me the unforgettable moment in which the Israeli Rabin and the Palestinian Arafat shake hands and assure one another that in the future they want to look not only at their own suffering, but also to remember the suffering of others, the suffering of their former enemies, and that they want to take this into consideration in their own actions. This really is the politics of peace from the biblical *memoria passionis* ! I know that agreement on this basis is extremely fragile, that it demanded and will demand great sacrifice. Doesn't this model a shared responsibility not driven by any totalitarianism of rights?

Doesn't such a vision of peace *ex memoria passionis*, from remembering others' suffering, also hold for other bloody conflicts today, for example, the civil wars based on cultural and religious conflicts in Lebanon and Ireland? And besides, only if there grows among us a political culture inspired by remembering others' suffering, will there also be a chance that Europe will be a blooming multicultural landscape and not a burning multicultural landscape, a landscape of peace and not a landscape of imploding violence, that is to say, not a landscape of escalating civil wars.

III

In the current discussion about a "global ethic" (Hans Küng) there is talk about a moral universalism which should emerge on the basis of a so-called minimal or basic consensus — "as the necessary minimum of common human values, criteria and basic attitudes."[2] But from a strictly theological and not just from a religious and political perspective, moral universalism is not a product of consensus. It is rooted in the acknowledgment of an authority which can now also be called upon in all great religions and cultures: the acknowledgment of the authority of those who suffer. Their authority refutes what sociologist Zygmunt Bauman says about conscience, namely, that it demands "obedience without proof that the command should be obeyed; conscience can neither convince nor coerce.... By the standards which support the modern world, conscience is weak."[3] Bauman's claim, however, does not apply to the authority of those who suffer. Their authority can no longer be shaped by hermeneutic or made safe by discussion. On the contrary, when obedience to discourse and communication has primacy over the authority of those who suffer, then the basis of all morality is lost.

In our technological and scientific world civilization, every ethics that doesn't want finally to become just an "ethics of accommodation," an

---

2. Hans Küng, *A Global Ethic for Global Politics and Economics* (1997; New York: Oxford University Press, 1998), 92.
3. Zygmunt Bauman, *Postmodern Ethics* (Oxford: Basil Blackwell, 1995), 249.

ethics of acceptance or justification, falls under this obedience. Such an ethics of accommodation no longer defines the goals and limits of human action but rather seeks to reconcile human action with ever-changing "practical circumstances." For example, where in such an ethic is there any objection to the looming form of biotechnology within which "the human being" is seen as a residue, a bit of nature in an unfinished experiment?

One shouldn't see this obedience as a welcome tool for the Church in her own demands for obedience. The Church itself stands not above this obedience, but under it. This obedience cannot therefore be glossed over by the Church. Actually it can become a basis for a profound critique of Church action itself. Hasn't the Church's proclamation of God almost forgotten that the biblical word of God is spelled out in the memory of others' suffering, that remembering the God of dogma must not be divorced from remembering the cries of a suffering humanity? Doesn't the crisis of God, which stands in the background of today's often-mentioned crisis of the Church, spring from an ecclesial praxis in which God was and is preached with our backs to the history of human suffering? Does the proclamation of God by the Church seem perhaps prone to fundamentalism because in it the authority of God is separated from the authority of the those who suffer — even though Jesus himself has, in his well-known parable of the last judgment (Matt. 25:31–46), put the entire history of humanity under the authority of those who suffer?

For me, therefore, this authority alone manifests the authority of the judging God in the world for all humanity. The moral conscience is formed by obedience to this authority, and what we call the voice of conscience is our reaction when the suffering of the other strikes home. We certainly need to be more precise about all this, more exact in defining those who suffer as innocent, as suffering unjustly. I have discussed this question often in one way or another, and have pointed out that the struggle for justice can generate a universal horizon only by its "negative mediation," only by resisting unjust suffering.

Isn't it resistance to unjust suffering, largely inspired by respect for the authority of those who suffer, which brings humankind together from quite diverse religious and cultural worlds? They do not really follow a theory or ideology of justice, but rather their convictions, convictions rooted in that obedience mentioned before to which, according to Paul (Rom. 2:14), all people, even pagans, are subject because of their human dignity. Here I see the opportunity and task for an ecumenism of religions that takes the form of an *indirect ecumenism of religions* — in accord with the thinking of the new political theology. This ecumenism is not a coming together and comparing religions, but the praxis of a common response, a common resistance to the sources of unjust suffering in the world: racism, xenophobia, and nationalistic or purely ethnic religiosity with its civil war ambitions. But it is also a resistance to the cold alternative of a global community in which increasingly the "human being" vanishes amid self-serving systems of economics, technology, and their culture and communications industries; of a global community in which world politics increasingly loses its primacy to a world economics whose laws of the market long ago abstracted from "human beings" themselves. "The world may be moving inexorably towards one of those tragic moments that will lead future historians to ask, why was nothing done in time? Were the economic and policy elites unaware of the profound disruption that economic and technological change were causing working men and women? What prevented them from taking the steps necessary to prevent a global social crisis?"

Who would call such sentences careless alarmism?[4] Where would one find those powers who could reclaim and defend in time the humane foundations of politics against the accelerating, pervasive, and autonomous laws of economics and technology? Is a new political subculture of civil society — now free to engage in a risky individualism — sufficient? Or is a global politics through such renowned institutional subgroups as Amnesty International, *Terre des hommes*, or Greenpeace sufficient? Aren't we dealing here with a situation in which worldwide, religiously based institutions should be more political than "normal" society? Isn't this the hour in which the world's religions, in the form of that indirect ecumenism outlined above, should intervene in politics, not in order to speak out for a dreamy liberal politics or even less for a fundamentalist religious politics, but rather to support a conscientious world politics in this hour of great danger? They will, of course, succeed only if they do not look to their own institutional interest in survival but to a fundamental interest in the suffering of others.

IV

Certainly this biblical religion of sensitivity to suffering speaks not primarily of a morality, but of a hope; its talk of God is not grounded in an ethics, but in an eschatology. It is true of both the world of religion and the world of morality that neither can tolerate the indifferent voyeur. One is not introduced to the world of religion by religious studies nor to

---

4. In fact this comes from Ethan Kapstein, director of the Washington Council of Foreign Relations, as cited in Hans-Peter Martin and Harold Schumann, *The Global Trap: Globalization and the Assault on Democracy and Prosperity* (London: Zed Books, 1997), 240.

the world of morality by ethics. Before one can develop a self-conscious relationship to them, one has to practice, one has to become, so to speak, biographically engaged. Morality and religion which deserve their names are grounded in communities of memory. And this goes also for those positions which place themselves in opposition to religion in the name of morality.

The fundamental connection of religion and morality with community and tradition does not dispense with the question of how and according to which criteria particular communities of memory should act toward one another in our one world, how they might avoid falling into an isolating relativism or a relativism checked only by force. This question, now being addressed to all so-called communitarian approaches, I have tried to answer throughout my recent book[5] where I put forth the notion of a *memoria passionis* which is at the same time both universalizable and particular: the memory of others' suffering. I develop this basic theological-political category in resistance to the cultural amnesia of our time.

Religion is essentially resistance to this cultural amnesia. This is especially so for Christianity. The Church as an institution is above all a collection of recollections, a long-term memory, an "elephant's memory" in which much, all too much, is stored: liberation and oppression, light and darkness. Theology does not stand apathetically outside or above this memory. It shows its critical competence when it questions the official, canonical memory of the Church. Theology asks whether and to what extent this memory has become in practice the memory of others' suffering; whether and to what extent the Church's memory of God and the dogmatic picture of Christ haven't long ago distanced themselves from the memory of human suffering, from the everyday *memoria passionis.*

Theology also puts this critical question to other monotheistic religions: Do they perhaps often seem so fundamentalist only because their memory of God long ago moved away from the memory of others' suffering? The new political theology insists that the dialogue of religions and cultures so rightly demanded today stand under the criterion of a *memoria passionis*, of a memory of others' suffering. The criterion for truth in this dialogue is bringing the suffering of others to expression. The "weak" memory of others' suffering and the narratives it forms can prove their power for interreligious and intercultural communication by bringing to expression the diverse histories of suffering in the world,

---

5. *Zum Begriff der neuen Politischen Theologie, 1967–1997* (Mainz: Matthias-Grünewald-Verlag, 1997), from which this chapter is drawn. This book represents a selection of the most important articles in the development of a new political theology. Many of the topics mentioned in this chapter are treated in more detail there.

as for example in the encounter of biblical religion with the ethics of compassion found in Asian religions.

How these two classical mysticisms of suffering deal with the suffering of others will be crucial. If I may use metaphorical abbreviation, in biblical religion it is primarily a matter of relating to the other, of a mysticism of suffering with the eyes open; in Buddhism it is primarily a matter of relating to the self, of a mysticism of suffering with the eyes closed. These two will be able to learn from each other only if they do not lose sight of their differing roots.

Of course the new political theology also turns its basic criterion to "profane" models and theories of social and cultural life. It critically inquires whether our posttraditional communities of discourse — having renounced the *a priori* of a (cultural) memory of suffering — really go beyond the anonymous power of the market, of exchange and competition; whether these communities still know about the responsibility of one for the other prior to any relationship of exchange or competition. This new political theology tries critically to break the spell of cultural amnesia, of the mindless presence of those virtual worlds created by our culture and communications technology. And it does this not for the sake of theology, but for the sake of humanity itself.

V Questions...

Finally, after all these abstract reflections I need to share one more persistent and troubling question. Does anyone at all want to hear about a Christianity with a heightened sensitivity to the suffering of others? Shouldn't religion shelter us from the pain of negativity? If anything, doesn't religion promote the triumph of the "positive"? Why else would it be called "good" news? And finally: Is not this sensitivity to suffering especially difficult for young people to accept? Can it even be made acceptable to them? I can only answer these and similar questions with a counter question: Whom should one see as able to attend to the suffering of others, as capable of this attitude of empathy and excess? From whom should one expect the strange notion of caring for others without getting something in return? Is there anyone at all to whom one might offer this "alternative way of life"? To whom shall we offer this, I ask, if not to these same young people? Have we totally and completely forgotten that Christianity first began as a youth revolt within the Jewish world?

Permissions

"The Church and the World," in T. Patrick Burke, ed., *The Word in History: The St. Xavier Symposium* (New York: Sheed & Ward, 1966), pp. 69–85. Reprinted with permission of Sheed & Ward, an Apostolate of the Priests of the Sacred Heart, Franklin, Wisconsin.

"The Church's Social Function in the Light of a 'Political Theology,' " Theodore L. Westow, translator, *Concilium* 36, pp. 2–18 (New York: Paulist Press: 1966). Reprinted with permission of Stichting Concilium, Nijemgen, Holland.

"Christians and Jews After Auschwitz: Being a Meditation also on the End of Bourgeois Religion," in *The Emergent Church* (New York: Crossroad, 1981). Reprinted with permission of The Crossroad Publishing Company.

"Bread of Survival: The Lord's Supper of Christians as Anticipatory Sign of an Anthropological Revolution," in *The Emergent Church* (New York: Crossroad, 1981). Reprinted with permission of The Crossroad Publishing Company.

"Theology Today: New Crises and New Visions," in *Proceedings of The Catholic Theological Society of America* 40 (1985): 1–14. Reprinted with permission of The Catholic Theological Society of America.

"Between Evolution and Dialectics," David Smith, translator, *Faith in History and Society* (London: Burns and Oates/Seabury, 1980), pp. 3–13. Reprinted with permission of Search Press Ltd.

"The Dangerous Memory of The Freedom of Jesus Christ," David Smith, translator, in *Faith in History and Society* (London: Burns & Oates/Seabury, 1980), pp. 88–99. Reprinted with permission of Search Press Ltd.

"A Short Apology of Narrative," David Smith, translator, *Concilium* 85, pp. 84–96 (New York: Herder & Herder, 1973). Reprinted with permission of Stichting Concilium.

"An Identity Crisis in Christianity," in William J. Kelly, S.J., ed., *Theology and Discovery: Essays in Honor of Karl Rahner, S.J.*, Marquette University Press, 1980, pp. 169–178. Reprinted with permission of Marquette University Press, Milwaukee, Wisconsin.

"Theology in the New Paradigm: Political Theology," Margaret Köhl, translator, in Hans Küng and David Tracy, eds., *Paradigm Change in Theology* (New York: Crossroad, 1989). Reprinted with permission of T & T Clark, Ltd., Edinburgh.

"Communicating a Dangerous Memory," in Fred Lawrence, ed., *Communicating a Dangerous Memory: Soundings in Political Theology*, Lonergan Workshop 6 (Atlanta: Scholar's Press, 1987), 37–53. Reprinted with permission of the Boston College Lonergan Workshop.

"The Second Coming," Thomas Linton, translator, in *Followers of Christ* (Paulist Press/Burns and Oates, 1977), pp. 75–83. Reprinted with permission of Search Press, Ltd.

"The Courage to Pray," Sarah O'Brien Twohig, translator, in *The Courage to Pray* (New York: Crossroad, 1981), pp. 5–28. Reprinted with permission of Search Press Ltd.

"In The Pluralism of Religious and Cultural Worlds: Notes Toward a Theological and Political Program," translated with permission by John K. Downey and Heiko Wiggers from *Zum Begriff der neuen Politichen Theology 1967–1997* (Mainz: Matthias-Grünewald-Verlag, 1997), pp. 197–206.

Index

Lightning Source UK Ltd.
Milton Keynes UK
171285UK00001B/224/P